Bibliotheca Indo-Buddhica Series No. 121

The Word - Index of *Abhidharmakośa*

Compiled by:
Shubhangi S. Pradhan

Sri Satguru Publications
A Division of
Indian Books Centre
Delhi • India

Published by :
Sri Satguru Publications
Indological and Oriental Publishers
A Division of
Indian Books Centre
40/5, Shakti Nagar,
Delhi-110007
(INDIA)

First Published 1993

ISBN 81-7030-369-9

Printed at :
D.K. Fine Art Press, Delhi.

PRINTED IN INDIA

अंश : aṁśa

VI.36

अकनिष्ठग : akaniṣṭhaga

VI.37

अकर्म : akarma

IV. 65

अकारगोचर : akāragocara

VII. 8

अकार्य : akārya

VI. 60

अकिंचन : akiṅcana

VIII. 4

अकिंचन्यसांमुख्य : akiṅcanyasāṁu-khya

VIII. 20

अकुरूकामिन् : akurukāmin

IV. 58

अकुशल : akuśala

II. 26

II. 29

II.31

IV. 9

V. 42

अकुशल : akuśala

II.66[2]

II. 67

अकुशल : akusal

IV.45

अकुशलमूल : akuśalamūla

V.20[2]

अकृत : akṛta

VII. 18

अकोप : akopa

IV. 111

अकोप्य : akopya

VI. 50

VI. 56

VI. 59

VI. 60

VII. 25

VIII. 27

अकोप्यधर्मन् : akopyadharman

VI. 56

VII. 36

अक्रियाप्तितस् : akriyātitas

IV. 33

अकिलष्ट : akliṣṭa

I. 40

II. 39

III. 4

V. 32

VIII. 13

अक्लिष्टव्याकृत : akliṣṭavyākṛta

I V. 98

- अक्ष : –aksa

III. 39

VI. 63

VII. 5

अक्ष : :aksa

III.14

-अक्षर- : –akṣara–

II. 47

अक्षरक्षण : akṣarakṣaṇa

III. 85

अक्षसंचारपरिहाणिभाक् : akṣasaṁcārapa r-ihāṇibhāk

VI. 41

अक्षाधिमोक्ष : akṣādhimokṣa

VII. 29

अक्षान्तिवध्या : akṣāntivadhyā

अक्षान्तिवध्य+आ (f)

V. 6

-अक्षि- : –akṣi–

VIII. 13

-अक्षित्- : –akṣit–

VI. 44

-अक्षिन्- : –akṣin–

III. 14

अक्षिन् : –:aksin

अक्षीणभावनाहेय : akṣīṇabhāvanā-heya

VI.34

-अक्षेम- : –akṣema–

IV. 45

अगत : agata

IV. 30

अगन्तुकामतामार्गविभ्रमः : agantukāmatām-ārgavibhramḥ

V. 44

अगम : agama

VI. 55

अगम्यगमन : agamyagamana

IV. 74

अगुरुता : agarutā (f)

II. 32

अग्नि : agni

III. 100

III. 102

अग्र : agra

IV. 52

IV. 117

V. 7

अग्र- : :–agra–

V. 16
V. 68
VI. 44
VI. 47
VII. 24

-अग्र : **–agra**
VI.45
VIII. 20

-अग्रग : **–agraga**
VI. 38

अग्रज : **agraja**
II. 39
II. 52
V.6

-अग्रज : **–agraja**

-अग्रजा : **–agrajā**
(f)
II. 43

अग्रधर्म : **agradharma**
VI. 21
VI.25
VI.27

अग्रधर्मा : **agradharmā**
(f)
VI. 19

-अग्रा : **–agrā**
(f)
III. 6

अग्र्य : **agrya**
VII.47

-अग्र्य : **–agrya**
VIII. 1

-अङ्ग्- : **–aṅga–**
VI. 73

-अङ्ग्ः- : **–aṅgaḥ–**
III. 20
III. 27

-अङ्ग् : **–aṅga**
IV. 29^3
VI. 71
VI. 72
VI. 75

अङ्गकारण : **aṅgakāraṇa**
IV. 36^2

अङ्ग्कीर्तन : **aṅgakīrtana**
III. 25

-अङ्ग्ता : **–aṅgatā**
IV. 116

अङ्ग्ना : **aṅganā**
(f)
VI. 21

अङ्.गुलि : **aṅguli**
III. 87

अङ्.गुलिपर्व : **aṅguliparva**
III. 86

अङ्ग्चतुष्टय : **aṅgacatuṣṭaya**
VIII. 7

अङ्ग्च्छेद : **aṅgaccheda**
IV. 111

अचरम : **acarama**
II. 62
IV. 48

-अचित्त- : **–acitta–**
II. 67
IV. 95

अचित्तक : **acittaka**
I.10

अज : **aja**
V. 24

अजात : **ajāta**
IV. 90

अजात : **:–ajāta**
VII. 5

-अजातनष्टता : **ajātanaṣṭatā**
V. 27

अजातय : **ajāntaya**
II. 39

अजाति : **ajāti**
IV. 20
IV. 23

अणु : **aṇu**
III. 85
IV. 3
V. 39

अण्डज : **aṇaḍaja**
III. 16

अण्डजादि : **aṇḍajādi**
III. 8

अत : **ata**
I. 3

अतः : **ataḥ**
I. 45

अत : **atas**
II. 31

अतः : **ataḥ**
IV. 47
IV. 77
IV. 115
V.8
V. 21
V. 36
V. 44
VI. 57
VII. 21

-अति- : **–ati–**
IV. 107

अतिक्रम : **atikrama**
V. 43
V. 68

अतिक्रान्तमनस्कार : **atikrāntamanas -kāra**
VI. 11

अतिगर्हयत्व : **atigarhyatva**
IV. 33

-अतिपात : **–atipāta**

IV. 73

अतिविध : **atividha**
IV. 85

अतिशय : **–atiśaya**
III. 97

अतिसेवन : **atisevana**
VI. 60

अतीत : **atita**
I. 17

अतीरण : **atiraṇa**
I. 41

अतीत : **atīta**
I. 44

अति+ इ
II. 59
IV. 19
IV. 20
IV. 23
IV. 24
IV. 90

अतीत- : **:–atita–**
IV.4

अतीतप्रत्युपस्थित : **atitapratyupast hita**
V. 23

अतीता : **atītā**
(f)
II. 39

अतुष्टि : **atuṣṭi**
(f)
VI. 6

अत्यन्त : **atyanta**
I. 6
IV. 55

अत्यन्तशान्ति : **atyantaśānti**
(f)
VI. 8

-अत्यय : **–atyaya**
IV. 38

अत्याग : **atyāga**
IV. 19
IV. 38

अतर्क : **atarka**
VIII. 22

अतद्वान् : **atadvān**
VIII. 14

अत्र : **atra**
I. 3
I. 29
II. 30
III. 3
III. 28
III. 36
III. 67
IV. 78
IV. 83
VI. 26

अत्रपा : **atrapā**
II. 32

अथ : **atha**
II. 34
III. 59
III. 93
IV. 93
IV. 96
IV. 112
V. 14
V. 40
V. 58
VI. 53
VII. 38
VIII. 42

अथवा : **athavā**
I. 23
V.66

अदत्तादान : **adattādāna**
IV. 73
IV. 70

-अदर्शित्व- : **–adarśitva–**
II. 32

अदस् : **adas**
III. 102[2]

अदुःख : **adakha**
VIII. 8
VIII. 23
VIII. 22

-अदुःखासुखवेद्य- : **–adukhāsukhav e-dya–**
IV. 47

अदृष्टतत्व : **adrṣṭatatva**
VIII. 41

अदृष्टदृष्टेर्दृङ्.मात्र : **adrṣṭadrṣṭerdrr-gmatra**
VI. 28

अद्वय : **advaya**
VIII. 23

-अद्रि- : **–adri–**
III. 57

अद्वेष : **adveṣa**
VIII. 29

अद्य : **adya**
II. 30
II. 31
VII. 32
VIII. 7
VIII.42

-अद्य- : **–adya–**
V.64
III.45

अधः : **adhaḥ**
III. 58

III. 72

अध : **adha**
III. 95
IV. 48
VII. 26
VIII. 15
VI. 47

-अध- : **–adha–**
VIII.23

अधस्ततः : **adhastataḥ**
III. 81

अधर : **adhara**
I. 46
I. 47
VI. 13
VII. 51
VIII. 19

अधर : **adhar**
V.30
VIII. 33

अधरक्रम : **adharakrama**
III.95

अधरगोचर : **adharagocara**
VI. 49
VIII. 21

अधरशुद्धक : **adharasuddhaka**
VIII. 16

अधिक : **adhika**
II. 28
II. 30
IV. 99[2]
IV. 101
III. 81

-अधिक : **:–adhika**
VII. 31

अधिकाधिक : **adhikādhika**
III. 81

-अधिगमात्मक : **–adhigamātma ka**
VIII. 39

अधिप : **adhipa**
II. 62

अधिपति : **adhipati**
II. 58

अधिपतिनिष्यन्दविपाकफलदा : **adhipatinisyand-avipākaphaldā**
IV. 85

-अधिमात्र : **–adhimātra**
VI. 33

अधिमात्रा : **adhimātrā**
(f)
VI.19

अधिमात्य : **adhimātrya**
VII. 33

अधिमुक्त : **adhimukta**
VI. 76

-अधिमुक्त- : **:–adhimukta**
VI.31

-अधिमुक्तिज : **:–adhimuktija**
V.56

अधिमोक्ष : **adhimokṣa**
II. 24
VII. 29

अधिमोक्ष :- : **adhimoksh**

अधिमोक्षिकी : **adhimokṣikī**
(f)
VII. 48

अधिरागवितर्क : **adhirāgavitarka**
VI. 9

अधिवचन : **adhivacana**
III. 30

अधिष्ठान : **adhiṣṭhāna**
IV. 71
IV. 119
VII. 52

अधिष्ठाय : **adhiṣṭhāya**
VII. 51

-अधो- : **–adho–**
VIII. 19

अधोनृसुरगा : **adhonṛsuragā**
III. 44

अधोभूमिविवेकज : **adhūbhumivive -kaja**
VIII. 2

अध्यात्म : **adhyātma**
I. 37

अध्यात्मिक : **adhyātmika**
I. 48

अध्यात्मिका : **adhyatmika**
I. 39

-अध्व- : **–adhva–**
V. 62

-अध्वग : **–adhvaga**
II. 55

अध्वन् : **adhvan**
I. 7
V.26

अध्वपर्यन्त : **adhvaparyanta**
III. 85

अध्वायोग : **adhvāyoga**
V. 27

-अध्विक : **–adhvika**
V. 24

-अननुग्रह : **–ananugraha**
III. 39

अनन्तर : anantara
I. 17
IV. 112
VIII. 15
VIII. 33

-अनन्तरम् : :–anantara
IV. 69
VIII. 18

अनन्तरम् : anantaram
II. 68[2]

अनन्त्य : anantya
VIII. 4

अनन्त्यविज्ञान : anantyavijñāna
VIII. 4

अनन्तर्य : anantarya
IV. 62

-अनन्तर्य- : –znantarya–
VI. 28

-अनन्तर्य : –anantarya
VI. 65

अनन्तर्यकारिन् : anantaryakārin
III. 44
IV. 80

अनन्तर्यपथ : anantaryapatha
VI. 44
VI. 49

अनन्तर्यपथा : anantaryapathā
(f)
VI. 60

अनन्तर्यपथाष्टक : anantaryapathā-ṣṭaka
IV. 61

अनन्तर्यप्रयुक्त : anantaryaprayukta
IV. 104

अनन्तर्यमार्गज : anantaryamārg-aja
IV. 18

अनपकारतः : anapakārataḥ
V.16

-अनपत्र- : –anapatra–
V. 47
V. 51

अनपत्रपा : anapatrapā
(f)
II. 26

अनपायग : anapāyaga
VI. 23

अनभ्रक : anabhraka
III. 77

अन्तःकल्प : antaḥkalpa
III. 91
III. 83

अनागत : anāgata
V. 24
VII. 20

अनागता : anagata
IV.90

अनागामिता : anāgāmitā
IV. 107

अनागामीन् : anāgamin
VI. 36

अनागम्य : anāgamya
IV. 18
VI. 47
VI. 71

अनागम्यफल : anāgamyaphala
V. 66

अनागम्यान्तरध्यानभूमिक : anāgamyāntara-dhyānabhūmika
VI. 20

अनात्मतः : anātmataḥ
VI. 16

अनात्मशून्यता : anātmaśūnyatā
VIII. 24

अनाथ : anātha
VIII. 42

अनादि : anādi
III. 19

अनापानस्मृत : anāpānasmṛta
VI. 9

अनाप्त : anāpta
अन+आप्

II. 37

अनार्य : anārya
IV. 118
VI. 21
VI. 58

अनास्रव : anāsrava
I. 4
I. 5
I. 31
II. 66
IV. 5
IV. 13
IV. 17
IV. 44
IV. 88
VI. 1
VI. 47
VI. 61
VI. 71
VII. 2
VIII. 5
VIII. 6
VIII. 14
VIII. 15
VIII. 21

-अनास्रव - :- anāsrava -
V. 14
V.30
V.31
VIII.17

अनास्रवक्षण : **anāsravakṣaṇa**
VII. 19

अनास्रवता : **anāsravatā**
IV. 26

अनास्रववियोगाप्तेर्भवाग्रविकलीकृत : **anāsravaviyogā-pterbhavāgravi-kalīkṛta**
V. 68

अनास्रवाप्ति : **anāsravāpti**
VI. 53

अनास्रवास्त्रिधात्वन्त्यत्रयानास्रवगोचर : **anāsravāstridhā-tvantyatrayānā s-ravagocara**
V. 31

अनिच्छावसन : **anicchāvasana**
III. 7

अनिञ्ज : **aniñja**
IV. 45
VIII. 11

अनिञ्जन : **aniñjana**
III. 101

अनित्यतः : **anityataḥ**
VIII.26

अनित्यता : **anityatā**
(f)
II. 45

अनित्यदुःखतः : **anityadukhataḥ**
VI. 16

अनिदर्शन : **anidarśana**
III. 11

अनिन्द्रिय : **aninindriya**
II. 22

अनिमित्त : **animitta**
VIII. 26

अनियत : **aniyata**
I. 47
III. 78

-अनियत :-**aniyata**
IV. 50

अनियता : **aniyatā**
(f)
II. 43

अनिवर्त्य : **anivartya**
III. 14

अनिवृत : **anivṛta**
II. 66
II. 68
II. 69
IV. 24
IV. 108

अनिवृत : **anivṛt**

अनिशाक्षय : **aniśākṣaya**
IV. 28

अनुनय : **anunaya**
III. 31

अन्वित : **anvita**

अनु+इ
II.17
II. 19^2
IV. 19
IV. 22
IV.25
IV. 72

अन्वित : **anvita**
VIII. 31

अनुकूलता : **anukūlatā**
IV.17^2
IV.23
V. 37

अनुक्रम : **anukrama**
IV.89
V.33

अनुगत : **anugata**
V.39

-अनुगुण : **–anuguṇa**
VIII. 17

-अनुग्रह : **–anugraha**
IV. 113

अनुत्तर : **anuttara**
IV. 127

अनुत्पत्तिधर्मक : **anutpattidhar-maka**
VII. 21

अनुत्पन्नकामाप्तसवस्तुक्लेशगोचर : **anutpannakāmā-ptasavastukleśa-gocara**
VII. 36

अनुत्पादक्षयज्ञान : **anutpādakṣaya-jñāna**
VI. 67
VII. 4

अनुत्पादधीः : **anutpādadhiḥ**
VII. 1

अनुत्पादमति : **anutpādamati**
(f)
VI. 50

अनुत्पादमतिर्मत : **anutpādamatir-mata**
VII. 7

-अनुपात्त- : **–anupātta–**
I. 34
IV. 6

अनुपात्तक : **anupattaka**
VI: 13

अनुपात्तिका : **anupāttikā**
IV. 5

-अनुपेततत्व : **–anupetatva**
III. 10

अनुबध्नन्ति : **anubadhnanti**
अनु + बन्ध्
V. 39

अनुबन्ध : **anubandha**
I. 10

अनुभव : **anubhava**
I. 14

अनुभूत : **anubhūta**
IV. 75

अनुभूयते : **anubhūyate**
अनु+ भू
IV. 56

अनुमानत : **anumānata**
III. 26

अनुवर्णित : **anuvarṇita**
(अनु + वर्ण्)
I. 26

अनुवर्तक : **anuvartaka**
IV. 10
IV. 11
IV. 12

-अनुवर्ति- : **–anuvarti–**
II. 50

-अनुवर्तिन् : **–anuvartin**
II. 51
IV. 17

अनुलोमित : **anulomita**
VII. 41

अनुलोम्यतः : **anulomyataḥ**
VI. 67

अनुवादिता : **anuvaditā**
IV. 28

अनुशय : **anuśaya**
V. 1
V. 17
V. 34
V. 35
V. 39

अनुशायक : **anuśāyaka**
V. 32

अनुशेरते : **anuśerate**
अनु+ शी
V.17
V. 39

-अनुसारिन् : **–anusārin**
VI. 29

अनुस्मरण : **anusmaraṇa**
I. 33

-अनृतादिवत् : **–anṛtādivat**
III. 28

अनेक : **aneka**
IV. 95
VII. 52

-अन्न : **–anna**
III. 37

-अन्त- : **:–anta–**
III. 25
V. 3
VII.45

अन्त : **anta**
V. 42
VI. 8
VII. 45
VIII. 8

अन्यगुप्ति : **anyagupti**
IV. 34

अन्तग्रहण : **antagrahaṇa**
V. 33

अन्तग्राह : **antagrāha**
V. 19

अन्त्याष्टक : **antyāṣṭaka**
II. 10

अन्तर्धित : **antardhita**
IV. 39

अन्धकारः : **andhakaraḥ**
I. 1

अन्तर : **antara**
I. 3
III. 10

अन्तर : **antara**
:
IV. 44

IV.48
IV. 100
VI. 41
VIII. 22

अन्तर : **antra**
II.31
III. 51
VJ.63
VI.72

अन्तरद्वीप : **antaradvipa**
III. 56

-अन्तर्मुख : **–antarmukha**
–V. 36

अन्तर्मुखत्व : **antarmukhatva**
V. 2

अन्तरा : **antarā**
III. 85

अन्तराभव : **anantarābhava**
III. 4
III. 9
III. 10
III. 40
IV. 53

अन्तराभवसंतति : **antarābhavasan-tati**
(f)
III. 18

अन्तराया : **antarāya**
V. 44

अन्तरित : **antarita**
I. 42
III. 68
IV. 103

अन्तरीभव : **antarībhava**
VII. 55

अन्तरोत्पन्नसंस्कारा-संस्कारपरिनिवृतिः : **antarotpannasaṁ-skārāsaṁskār aparinirvṛti**
VI. 37

अन्ते : **ante**
III. 78
IV. 102

अन्त्य : **antya**
I. 32
I. 40
II. 16
II. 42
II. 56
IV. 17
IV. 62
V. 31
IV. 24
VI. 55
VII. 21
VII. 36
VIII. 28
VIII. 32
VIII. 36

अन्त्यज : **antyaja**
IV. 110

अन्त्यजन्मन् : **antyajanman**
IV. 118

अन्यतः : **anyataḥ**
VI. 45

अन्त्यनवमी : **antyanavamī**
III. 61

अन्तयमुक्ति : **antyamukti**
(f)
VII. 25

अन्त्या : **antyā**
(f)
VI. 48

(अन्त्य+आ)
VI. 59

अन्य : **anya**
VI. 59
VI. 78
VII. 6
VII. 12²
VII. 14
VII. 31
VII. 35
VII. 39
VII. 41
VII. 48
VIII. 31
VIII. 35
VI.28

-अन्य- : **:–anya–**

अन्यम् : **anyam**

अन्य : **anya**
II. 11
II. 31
II. 50
II. 52

अन्य : **anya**
II. 63
II. 65
V.II. 6
III. 15
III. 16

अन्य : **anya**
V. 65
VII. 1

अन्यकामवेद्य : **anyakāmavedya**
IV. 63

अन्यतस् : **anyatas**
IV. 28

-अन्यतादिवत् : **–anyatādivat**
V.22

अन्यत् : **anyat**
I. 23
II. 11
III. 36
IV. 7
IV. 77
IV. 87
V. 27
VII.15
VII. 18
VII. 55

अन्यत्कृष्णशुक्ल : **anyatkṛṣṇaśukla**
IV. 63

अन्यत्र : **anyatra**
II. 8
II. 30
III. 72
IV. 83
IV. 100
V. 33
VI. 72

-अन्यत्र : **:–anyatra**
II.66

अन्यथा : **anyathā**
I.16
I. 43
V. 26
VI. 4
VII. 10

-अन्यथा- : **:– anyathā**
V: 26

अन्यथासंज्ञिन् : **anyathāsaṁjñin**
IV. 74

-अन्यथिक- : **–anyathika–**

ya

VIII. 25

अपवादिन् : **apavādin**

IV. 79

अपह्रास : **apahrasa**

III. 98

-अपरान्त : **–aparanta**

III. 20

अप् : **ap**

I. 12
III. 46

-अप्- : **:–ap–**

III. 86

अपि : **api**

I. 1
I. 5
I. 8
I. 10
I. 13
I. 19
I. 27
I. 38
I. 40
I. 43
II. 13
II. 31
II. 48
II. 61
III. 9
III. 16^2
III. 64
IV. 7
IV. 8
IV 12
IV. 20
IV. 30
IV.43
IV. 44
IV. 48
IV. 52^2
IV. 65
IV. 67
IV. 83
IV. 84
IV. 90
IV. 92
IV. 102
IV. 103
IV. 111
IV. 118
IV. 121
V. 11
V. 13^2
V. 39
V. 46^2
V. 51
V. 56
VI. 17
VI. 18
VI. 20
VI. 23
VI. 42
VI. 44
VI. 74
VII. 23
VII. 48
VII. 50
VII. 52
VII. 55
VIII. 4
VIII. 15
VIII 26
VIII. 29
VIII. 38

-अपि- : **:–api–**

VIII.23

-अपुण्य : **apuṇya**

–IV. 45

अपूर्व : **apūrva**

II. 58
IV. 48

अपूर्वाप्ति : **apūrvāpti**

(f)
VI. 22

-अपोह : **–apoha**

VI. 4

अपोहय : **apohya**

II. 12

अप्रणिहित : **apranṣihita**

VIII. 24

अप्रतिघ : **apratigha**

I. 37
V. 5

अप्रतिघवत् : **apratighavat**

III. 14

अप्रतिसंख्या : **apratisaṁkhyā**

(f)
I. 6

-अप्रत्यागति : **–apratyāgati**

VI. 40

अप्रमाण : **apramāṇa**

VIII. 29

अप्रमाद : **apramāda**

II. 25

अप्रयुक्त : **aprayukta**

VI. 32

अप्रयोग : **aprayoga**

VIII. 4

-अप्रयोगतः : **–aprayogataḥ**

VII. 6

अप्रहीण : **aprahīṇa**

V. 23
V. 34

अप्रहेय : **apraheya**

IV. 94

अप्राप्त : **aprāpta**

I. 43

-अप्राप्त- : **–aprapta–**

VI. 59

अप्राप्ति : **aprāpti**

–अमल : —amalā
IV- 127
V- 30
IV 4
III. 92
VI. 27
VIII. 40

–अयस्– : –ayas–
III. 95

अयोगविहित : ayogavihita
IV. 94

अयोनिश : ayoniśa
V. 34

अरणा : araṇā
(f)
VII. 36

–अरणा : –aranā–
IV. 56

अरणाप्रणिधिज्ञानप्रतिसंविद्गुणादि: : araṇāpraṇidhij-ñānapratisanivi-dguṇādi
(f)
VII. 35

अरादि : arādi
VI. 54

-अरूप : -arupa
I. 29
IV. 42

–अरुप– : —arupa—
II. 66

–अरुप : —arupa
IV- 42

अरूपिणस्त्रय : arupiṇastraya
III. 5

अरूपिन् : arupin
III. 30
IV. 44
VI. 72
VIII. 34

अरूपिसामन्तक : arupisāmaṁtaka
III. 35

अरूप्य : arupya
V. 5

अर्क : arka
III. 60

–अर्क– : —arka—
III. 73

अर्कसामीप्य : arkasāmīpya
III. 62

अर्णव : arṇava
I. 3

अर्थ : artha
I. 9
IV. 41
VI. 5

–अर्थ : —arthas
I- 14
VI. 42
VII. 37

अर्थाभिज्ञ : arthābhijña
IV. 74

अर्थचर्या : arthacaryā
(f)
VII. 34

अर्थतस् : arthatas
I. 2

–अर्थ्य : —arthya
I. 23

अर्थयोग : arthayoga
I. 22

–अर्थवत् : —arthavat
VI. 34

अर्थसंवित् : arthasaṁvit
(f)
VII. 39

अर्ध : ardha
I. 34
III. 60
III. 81

अर्ध– : —ardha—
III. 83
III. 66
III. 77

अमला : amalā
(f)
I. 2
VII. 1

अमार्ग : amārga
V. 7

अमित : amita
III. 78
III. 91

–अमित्र– : —aṁitra—
III. 28

अमुकातत्व : —amuktatva—
VIII. 11

अमेय : ameya
IV. 118

अम्बु : aṁbu
III. 100

अयम्
इदम् (पुं) : ayam
III. 27

I. 9
I. 1
I. 15
IV. 4
IV. 5
IV. 7[2]
IV. 13
IV. 19
IV. 22
IV. 25
IV. 37
IV. 67
IV. 68

अविज्ञप्ती : avitarka
IV. 16

अवितर्क : avitarka
IV. 57

अविद्यसंतति : avidyasantati
(f)
VII. 46

अविधा : avidyā
(f)
III. 21
V. 1
V. 12
V. 14

V. 20
V. 21
V. 36
VII. 45

–अविद्या– : —avidya—
III. 28

अविघ्यातः : avidyātaḥ
V. 48

अविद्येतर : avidyetara
III. 31

अविपर्यय : avipryaya
IV. 121

–अविरोधित्व : —avirodhitva
II. 30

अविरोधिन् : avirodhin
IV. 14

अविवर्त्य : avivartya
VII. 38

अवीच : avica
III. 83

अवीचि : avīci
(f)
III. 58

अवीची : avīci
IV. 99

–अवेणिक : —aveṇika
VII. 28

अवेणिकी : aveṇikī
V. 12

–अवेत्य– : —avetya—
VI. 73

अव्यक्ष : avyakṣa
IV. 108

अव्याकृत : avyākṛta
I. 29
II. 30
II. 38
II. 39
II. 47
II. 57
II. 72
III. 4
IV. 7
IV. 9
IV. 88
IV. 89
V. 19
V. 52

VII. 45
VII. 53
VIII. 13

अव्याकृतान्तमुख : avyākṛtāntamu-kha
V. 36

अव्याभिचारित्वाद्धितेष्टफलयोजना : avyabhicāritvād-hiteṣṭaphalayoj-ana
(f)
VII. 47

अव्याहत : avyāhata
VII. 30

–अशब्द : —aśabda
II. 22

अशातृ : aśātṛ
II. 7
II. 8

अशीति : aśīti
I. 25
III. 93

अशीतिसहस्रक : aśītisahasraka
III. 50
III. 95

असाधारणत्वात् : **asādhāraṇatvat**
I. 45

-असामन्तक : **—asāmantaka**
III. 35

-असाम्य- : **—asāmya—**
III. 11

-असिद्धत्व- : **—asiddhatva—**
III. 11

असुख : **asukha**
VIII. 8
VIII. 23

-असुख : **—asukha**
VIII. 22

-असुखवेद्य : **—asukhavedya**
IV. 47

असौ : **asau**
अदस् (स्त्री)
III. 13
अदस् (पुं०)
III. 52
इदम् (पुं०)
IV. 100
VI. 35
VI. 45
VI. 57
VII. 39

अस्तंगमन : **astaṅgamana**
III. 60

अस्त्यतः : **astyataḥ**
VI. 32

-अस्त्रजित् : **—astrajit**
III. 96

असन्तान : **asantāna**
III. 12

अस्मद् : **asmat**
VIII. 40

अस्मात् : **asmāt**
इदम् (पुं)
II. 70

अस्य : **asya**
I. 2
I . 46
III. 54
III. 58
III. 63
V. 37
VII. 30

-अस्थान : **—asthāna**
III. 3
VII. 28

-अस्तिता : **—astitā**
V. 25

अस्थिर : **asthira**
IV. 32
VII. 52

अस्मिता : **asmitā**
V.II

अस्मिन् : **asmin**
(इदम् - (पुं०)
I. 2

अस्ति : **asti**
(अस्)
I. 3
III. 12
III. 18
III. 72
III. 80
III. 101
IV. 7
IV. 8
IV. 21
IV. 23
IV. 27
IV. 30
IV.48
IV. 72
IV. 78
IV. 80

-अस्ति- : **—asti—**
V. 7
VI. 58
VII. 12
VII. 52
V. 7

-अस्तिवाद : **—astivāda**
V. 252

अस्वीकार : **asvīkāra**
V. 18

-अहत : **—ahata**
VI. 123

-अहन् : **—ahan**
III. 83

अहर् : **ahar**
III. 61

-अहर्- : **—ahar—**
III. 62

अहिंसा : **ahiṁsā**
II. 25

अहीनभावनाहेय : **ahīnabhāvanāh-eya**
VI. 29

अहेतु : **ahetu**
V. 7

अहेय : **aheya**
II. 38

अहोरात्र : **ahorātra**
III. 79
III. 80
III. 82
IV. 27[2]

अहोरात्रमास : **ahorātramāsa**

III. 89

अहोरात्र : **ahorātra**
IV. 272

अऱ्ली : **ahrli**
(f)
II. 32

आ : **ā**
III. 24

आकपालार्धत्याग : **ākapālāradhaty-āga**
VI. 10

–आकरण : **—ākaraṇa**
VI. 18

–आकाङ्.क्षा : **—ākaṅkṣā**
V. 32

आकार : **ākāra**
VII.8
VII.12
VII. 8
VIII.30

–आकार : **—ākāra**
VI. 53
VII. 33

–आकार : **—ākāra**
VI. 17
VII. 10
VII. 11
VII. 12
VII. 13²
VII. 21
VII. 33
VIII. 12
VIII. 30

आकारयन्ति : **ākārayanti**
आ+कृ
VII. 13

–आकारा : **—ākāra**
(f)
II. 34

आकार्यते : **ākaryate**
आ+कृ
VII. 13

आकाश : **ākāśa**
I. 5
I. 28
VIII. 4

आकीर्णभावित : **ākīrṇabhāvita**
VII. 23

आकीर्यते : **ākīryate**
आ+कृ
VI. 42

आकुल : **ākula**
VIII. 41

–आकृति : **—ākṛti**
(f)
III. 53
IV. 43

आक्षिपति : **ākṣipati**
आ+क्षिप्
IV. 53
IV. 95

आक्षिपते : **ākṣipate**
आ+क्षिप्
IV. 109

आक्षिप्यते : **ākṣipyate**
आ+क्षिप्
VI. 25

–आक्षेप : **—ākṣepa**
III. 13
III. 19
III. 41
IV. 51

आक्षेपण : **ākṣepaṇa**
IV. 51

आक्षेपिक : **ākṣepīka**
IV. 95

आक्ष्य : **ākṣya**
VIII. 28

आख्य : **ākhya**
I. 15
II. 4
II.54
II. 57

–आख्य – : **—ākhya—**
VII.21

–आख्य : **—ākhya**
I. 24
I. 28
II. 43
II. 49
II. 61
II. 62
III. 4
IV. 13
IV. 14
IV. 18
IV. 26
V. 61
VI. 1
VI. 13
VI. 27
VI. 65
VI. 69
VIII. 3

आख्या : **ākhyā**
(f)
VI. 46

–आख्या : **—ākhyā**
II. 44
II. 47
IV. 6
VI. 78
VII. 46

आख्यात : **ākhyāta**

VI. 1

आगः : āgaḥ
VIII. 40

—आगम : —āgama
VIII. 9

आगमाधिगमात्मक : āgamadhigamā-tmaka
VIII. 39

आगम्य : āgamya
VIII. 18

आगामीन् : āgāmin
VI. 35

—आचार : —ācāra
IV. 33
IV. 74

आच्छेद्यलाभितृ : ācchedyalābhitṛ
IV. 115

आज्ञा : ājñā
II. 19

आज्ञाख्यम् : ājñākhyam
II. 4

आज्ञात : ājñāta
II. 4
II. 19

आज्ञातेन्द्रिय : ājñātendriya
(f)
II. 19

आज्ञास्यामि (आ + ज्ञा) : ājñāsyāmi
II. 4
II. 19

—आतृतीया : —ātṛtīyā
IV. 47

—आत्म— : —ātma—
V. 8

—आत्मक : —ātmaka
III. 39
VI. 7

—आत्मतः : ātmataḥ
VII. 18

आत्मन् : —ātman
III. 18

आत्मविवर्जित : ātmavivarjita
VII. 12

—आत्मा— : —ātmā—
V. 22

आत्मात्मीयध्रुवोच्छेदना-स्तिहीनाग्रदृष्टि : ātmātmīyadhru-vocchedanāstih i- nāgradrṣti
(f)
V. 7

—आत्मीय— : —ātmīya—
V. 7

आत्याग : ātyāga
IV. 23

—आदन— : —ādana—
VII. 18

आदय : ādaya
II. 36

—आदय : —ādaya
I. 9
III. 59
IV. 9
IV. 88
IV. 89
IV. 93
VII. 28
VIII. 7

—आदर— : —ādara—
IV. 37

—आदादि— : —ādādi—
VI. 10

—आदान— : —ādāna—
IV. 37
IV. 41

—आदान : —ādāna
IV. 73

आदि : ādi
IV. 21
VII. 56
VIII. 17

—आदि : —ādi
I. 6
I. 12
II. 5
IV. 21
IV. 59
IV. 65
IV. 116
V. 4
V. 10
V. 41
VI. 33
VII. 3^2
VII. 7
VII. 31
VII. 54
VII. 56
VIII. 17
VIII. 29
VIII. 34

—आदि : —ādi
I. 39
I. 44
I. 45
II. 4
II. 23

I. 18
I. 20
I. 24
I. 27

-आयतन- : :–ayatana–
VII.31

-आयतन : :–ayatana–
I.14
III.39
VII. 49
I.15
III.22
III.39

आयस : āyasa
III. 49

आयुस् : āyus
II. 20
II. 45
III. 78
III. 79
III. 80
III. 82
III. 92
VII.34
III. 82

-आयुस् : –āyus
III. 84^2
III.91
III. 98
IV. 41

-आयुस्- : –āyus–
VII. 34

आरूप्य : ārupya
I. 31
II. 69
III. 34
III. 38
III. 81
IV. 84
V. 66

-आरूप्य- : :–ārupya–
VIII.38

-आरूप्य : –ārupya
VIII. 19
II.20
V.35
VIII. 21
VIII. 32
VIII. 36
VIII. 38

आरूप्यग : ārupyaga
VI. 38

आरूप्यजास्त्रिधात्वात्र-त्रयानास्रवगोचरः : ārupyajāstridhā -tvāpratrayānā sr- avagocara
V. 30

आरूप्यधातु : ārupyadhātu
III. 3

आरूप्यसंज्ञ : ārupyasaṁjña
VIII. 37

आरूप्या : ārupyā
VIII. 2

आरूप्याप्त : ārupyaptā
II. 12
IV. 40

आर्य : ārya
II. 21
II. 42
II. 43
III. 44
IV. 20
IV. 25
IV. 40
IV. 52
V. 11
VI. 21
VI. 48
VIII. 20
VIII. 22

-आर्य : –ārya
VIII. 33
VI.41

आर्यमार्ग : āryamārga
V. 67

आर्यमार्गस्थ : āryamārgastha
IV. 21

आर्यवंश : āryavaṁśa
VI. 7

आर्यवैराग्य : āryavairāgya
VI. 46

आर्यसत्व : āryasattva
IV. 17

आर्या : āryā
IV. 26

-आलम्ब- : –ālaṁba–
VI. 27
–VII. 37–

-आलम्ब : –alaṁba
VIII. 20

आलम्बन : ālaṁbana
II. 62
IV. 49
V.61

-आलम्बन : :–alaṁbana
VI. 16

आस्रवादि : **āsravādi**
V. 40

आस्वादन : **āsvādana**
VIII. 6

आस्वादनवत् : **āsvādanavat**
VIII. 5

आस्वाद्य : **āsvādya**
VIII. 6

आहार : **āhāra**
III. 39
III. 40

-आहार- : **–ahara**
V. 59

आहारस्थितिक : **āhārasthitika**
III. 38

आहुः : **āhuḥ**
ब्रू
III. 88

आहय : **āvhaya**
आ+व्हे
III. 30

अवहय : **avhaya**
III. 75

आहीक्यमनपत्राप्य-मीर्ष्येमर्त्सामाद्धव : **āhrīkyamanapa -trāpyamīrṣyā ma-tsaryamuddhava**
V. 47

आहीक्यानपत्राप्यस्त्यान-मिद्धोद्धवा : **āhrīkyānapatrā -pyastyānamidh -odhavā**
V. 51

आहीक्यौद्धत्यमत्सर : **āhrīkyoudhaty amatsara**
V. 48

-इच्छ : **–iccha**
IV. 104

इच्छा : **icchā**
(f)
II. 42

-इच्छा- : **–icchā–**
V.11

-इच्छा- : **-icchā-**
VI. 6
VI. 8

इञ्ज : **iñjā**
IV. 46

इञ्जति : **iñjati**
इञ्
IV. 46

इतर : **itara**
IV. 13
VI. 23
VI. 64
VI. 66
VI. 71

इतरा : **itarā**
VII. 45

-इतरत्- : **–itarat–**
IV. 45

-इतरत् : **–Itarat**
V.45

इति : **iti**
I. 2
I. 25
I. 26
II. 36
III. 19
III. 88
III. 92
IV. 32
IV. 39
IV. 49
IV. 51
IV. 77
V. 3
V. 5
V. 21
V. 33
V. 36
V. 38
V. 40
V. 44
V. 50
VI. 2
VI. 20
VI. 27
VI. 46
VI. 55
VII. 53
VIII. 5
VIII. 30
VIII. 43

इत्यादि : **ityādi**
VII. 7

इन्द्रिय : **indriya**
I. 20
I. 48
II. 2
II. 3
II. 4
II. 5
II. 6
II. 7
II. 12
VI.62

-इन्द्रिय- : **indriya**
IV. 18

V. 63

न्द्रिय : –indriya–
II.2
II.7
II.18
II.19
II.22
VI. 29
VI. 31
VI. 39

न्द्रियफल : indriyaphala
VI. 64

न्द्रियार्थ : indriyārtha
I. 14

न्द्रियोपेत : indriyopeta
II. 19

द्ध : iddha
V. 47
V. 51

द्धानपत्रप : iddhānapatrapa
V. 48

यम्
दम् (स्त्री) : iyam
II. 43

इव : iva
V. 62

इष्ट : iṣṭa
III. 42
V. 25
VII. 46
VII. 47

इष्टफलता : iṣṭaphalatā
IV. 121

इष्टा : iṣṭā
III. 25

इष्यते : iṣyate

इष्
II. 40
II. 49
III. 36
IV. 2
IV. 39
IV. 48
IV. 71
IV. 97

इह : iha
III. 10
III. 41
III. 57
III. 78
IV. 47
IV. 80
V. 19
VI. 38
VI. 55
VIII. 40
VIII. 42

-ईक्षित- : –īkṣita–
–III. 69–

ईरणा : īraṇā
I. 12

ईशाधार : īśādhāra
III. 48

ईश्वरादि : īśvarādi
II. 64
V. 8

ईर्ष्या : īrṣyā
(f)
II. 27
V. 42
V. 57

-ईर्ष्या- : –īrṣyā–
V. 47

ईर्ष्या : īrṣyā
V. 49

- ई ह न : –īhana
IV. 37

उक्त
(वच्) : ukta
I. 22
I. 27
II. 61
III. 36
II. 10

उक्त : ukta
II. 17
III. 4
IV. 28
IV. 75
V. 2
V. 42
VI. 2
VIII. 37

उक्ता
उक्त + आ : uktā
(f)
IV. 66
V. 38
VI. 75

उक्ति : ukti
(f)
IV. 30
VII. 46

-उक्ति- : –ukti–

IV. 4

-उक्ति- : **–ukti–**
III.12²
IV.59

उक्तत्व : **uktatva**
V. 25

उचिता : **ucitā**
(f)
VII. 44

-उच्छेदन- : **–ucchedana–**
–V. 7–

उच्यते : **ucyate**
I. 11
I. 13
I. 24
IV. 15
IV. 120

उज्जहार : **ujjahāra**
I. 1

उत्कर्ष : **utkarṣa**
III. 91
III. 92

उत्क्रान्त : **utkrānta**
VII. 5

उत्तप्त : **uttapta**
III. 97

उत्तापनमुक्ति : **uttāpanamukti**
VII. 24

उत्तापनागत : **uttāpanāgata**
VI. 57

-उत्तप्ति- : **–uttapti–**
IV. 40

-उत्तर : **–uttara**
VI.49
VIII.16
II. 14
III. 33
III. 57
II. 4
III. 68
III. 80
III. 84
III. 88
VI. 45
VI. 46
VIII. 6

उत्तरोत्तर : **uttarottar**
II. 4

-उत्तरग : **–uttaraga**
–III. 62

उत्तरमन्त्रिन् : **uttaramantrin**
III. 56

-उत्थ : **–uttha**
IV. 86
V. 48

-उत्थान- : **–utthāna–**
–IV. 10–

उत्थापक : **utthāpaka**
VIII. 13

-उत्थित : **–utthita**
IV. 56

उत्पत्ति : **utpatti**
(f)
II. 6
VI.15

-उत्पत्ति- : **–utpatti–**
IV. 79
VIII.17
V. 22
VI. 15

-उत्पत्ति- : **–utpatti–**
VI. 17
VIII. 3
VIII. 17
IV.38
V.22
VI.17
VIII.3

उत्पत्तिलाभिक : **utpattilābhika**
VII. 56

उत्पद्यते : **utpadyate**
उत्+पद्
VIII. 15

उत्पद्यवेधकृत् : **utpadyavedyakṛ**
IV. 52

उत्पन्न : **utpanna**
II. 62
IV. 25
V. 23
VIII.20
VI. 37

-उत्पन्न- : **–utpanna–**
VII. 20

उत्पाद : **utpāda**
I. 6
III. 22

-उत्पाद- : **–utpāda–**
VI. 8

-उत्पादन : **–utpādana**
VIII. 38

उत्पादबलध्यान : **utpādabaladhy-āna**
VII. 30

उदय : **udaya**
III. 60
III. 101

-उदय- : –udaya–
V.63
VII.42

-उदय : –udaya
IV. 41
IV. 42
IV. 72
V. 60
V. 63
VII. 42

उदार : udāra
VI. 49
IV. 115

-उदार- : –udāra–

उदित : udita
I. 3
V. 41
VII. 4

-उदित : –udita

-उदिता : –uditā
(f)
VI. 76

उद्ग्रहणात्मिका : udgrahaṇātmikā
(f)
I. 14

-उद्देश- : –uddeśa–
IV. 15

उद्धव : uddhava
II. 26

-उद्धव : –uddhava
V. 47

उद्धवा : uddhavā
V. 51

-उद्धार- : –uddhāra–
III. 84

उन्नति : unnati
II. 33

उद्भव : udbhava
I. 19
II. 57
III.94
VII.46
II.57
III. 42
III. 86
III. 93
IV. 103

उद्वेध : udvedha
III. 45
III. 46

-उनरात्र : –unarātra
–III. 89

-उपकार- : –upakāra–
–IV. 97–

उपकारिगुणक्षेत्रनिराकृतिविपादन : upakāriguṇakṣe-tranirākṛtivipād-ana
IV. 103

-उपकारित्व- : –upakāritva–
–IV. 117–

उपक्लेश : upakleśa
V. 46
V. 54

-उपक्लेशदेशन : –upakleśadeśana
–III. 29

-उपग : –upaga
–VI. 39
VI. 41

-उपगम : –upagama
–IV. 30

उपगृह्णन्ति : upagṛhaṇti
उप + ग्रह
V. 40

उपचयत: : upacayataḥ
VII. 8

-उपचित : –upacita
–IV. 20

उपनाह : upanāha
V. 50
V. 57

-उपनाह : upanāha
II. 27

उपनाहविहिंसन : upanāhavihiṁs-ana
V. 50

उपपत्ति : upapatti
(f)
III. 3
III. 13
VII. 55
VIII.1

-उपपत्ति : –upapatti
III.10
III. 42
III. 71[2]
VI. 43
VIII. 12

उपपत्तिज : upapattija
VII. 53

उपपत्तितः : **upapattitaḥ**
VIII. 14^2

उपपत्तिभवः : **upapattibhavaḥ**
III. 38

उपपत्तिविहारार्थ : **upapattivihārar-tha**
VI. 42

उपपत्याप्त : **upapatyāpta**
II. 71

उपपद्य : **upapadya**
II. 42

-उपपन्न- : **–upapanna–**
–III. 10–

उपपर : **upapara**
II. 15

उपपादुक : **uppāduka**
II. 14
III. 9

उपभोगतः : **upabhogataḥ**
VI. 59

-उपम : **–upama**
–III. 70^2
VI. 44

उपरत : **uparata**
IV. 102
V. 15

-उपरम : **–uparama**

-उपलब्ध : **–upalabdha**
–II. 2

उपवास : **upavāsa**
IV. 28
IV. 30

-उपवासस्थ- : **–upavāsastha–**
IV. 15

उपशान्ति : **upśānti**
(f)
I. 3

उपस्थान : **upasthāna**
VII. 16
VII. 44

-उपस्थान : **–upasthana**
:
VI.16

उपस्थानभावना : **upasthānabhāv-anā**
(f)
VI. 14

उपस्थिति : **upasthiti**
VI. 68

-उपात्त- : **–upātta–**
IV. 6

उपादान : **upādāna**
III. 23
V. 38

उपादानस्कन्ध : **upādānaskandha**
I. 8

उपादाय : **upādāya**
I. 11
IV. 5

उपासक : **upāsaka**
IV. 15

उपासकत्वोपगम : **upāsakatvopag-ama**
IV. 30

उपासकोपवासस्थश्रमणोद्देशभिक्षुता : **upāsakopavāsas-thaśramaṇodd-eś-abhikṣutā**
IV. 15

उपेक्षण : **upekṣaṇa**
VI. 68
VIII. 10

उपेक्षा : **upekṣā**
(f)
II. 8
II. 15
II. 17
II. 20
II. 25
III. 42
V. 56
V. 58
VIII. 8
VIII. 11^2
VIII. 12
VIII. 30

-उपेक्षा : **–upekṣā**

उपेक्षासुमनस्कता : **upekṣāsumanas-ktā**
(f)
VIII. 12

उपेक्षास्मृतिशुद्धि : **upekṣāsmṛtiśud-dhi**
(f)
VIII. 10

उपेक्षास्मृतिसमाधि : **upekṣāsmṛtisa-mādhi**
VIII. 8

-उपेत : **–upeta**
–II. 19

उभ : **ubha**
I. 43
I. 46

उभय : **ubhaya**
III. 17
III. 80
IV. 11
IV. 12
IV. 32
V. 42

उपेक्षा : –upekṣā
VI. 5

उभय : –ubhaya
IV.35
IV.60

भयतः : ubhayataḥ
VI. 63

भयतोविमुक्त : ubhayatovimukta
VI. 64

भयथा : ubhayathā
V. 58

भयाकरण : ubhayākaraṇa
VI. 18

भयार्थ : ubhayārtha
IV. 114

उभयार्थ : –ubhayartha
IV.114

भयार्था : ubhayārthā
(f)
VII. 1

भयवर्जित : ubhayavarjita
I. 32

उभयव्यञ्जनोत्पत्ति : ubhayavyañjan-otpatti
IV. 38

उभयी : ubhayī
(f)
II. 8

उषित : uṣita
III. 65

उष्णता : uṣṇata
(f)
I. 12

उशन्ति वश् : uśanti
III. 45

ऊर्ध्व : ūrdhva
I. 46
III. 2
III. 50
III. 58
II.69
III. 72[2]
III.77
III. 80
IV. 4
IV. 19
IV. 21
IV. 23
IV. 104
V. 19
V. 64
VI. 30
VI. 47
VI. 48
VI. 55
VII. 19
VII. 22
VII. 23
VIII. 15

-उर्ध्व- : –urdhva–
VI.48
VIII. 17
VIII. 34

उर्ध्वक : urdhvaka
V.30

उर्ध्वालम्बना : ūrdhvālaṁbanā
V. 13

ऊर्ध्वग : ūrdhvaga
III. 35

ऊर्ध्वज : ūdhvaja
IV. 46
VI. 41
VII. 50

ऊर्ध्वजन्मतस् : ūrdhvajanmatas
IV. 42

ऊर्ध्वदुःखादिगोचर : ūrdhvadukhādi dgocara
VII. 3

ऊर्ध्ववादः : ūrdhvavādaḥ
III. 15

ऊर्ध्वभागीय : ūrdhvabhāgīya
V. 45

ऊर्ध्वभूमिक : ūrdhvabhūmika
V. 56

ऊर्ध्वविषय : ūrdhvaviṣaya
V.18

ऊर्ध्ववृत्त : ūrdhvavṛtta
V. 21

ऊर्ध्वस्रोत : ūrdhvasrota
VI. 37
VI. 40

ऊष्म : ūṣma
II. 45
VI. 17

ऊष्मगतोत्पत्ति : ūṣmagatotapatti
(f)
VI. 17

-ऋतु- : –Ṛtu–
–IV. 116–

ऋते : Ṛte
II. 10

V. 35
V. 38
V. 45
V. 64
VI. 3
VI. 22
VI. 26
VI. 41
VI. 43
VI. 54
VI. 70
VI. 76
VI. 78
VII. 2
VII. 4
VII. 14
VII. 20
VII. 32
VII. 37
VII. 51
VIII. 19
VIII. 31
VIII. 39

एष **: eṣa**
एतद् (पुं)
I. 3

एषाम् **: eṣām**
(इदम् पुं)
I. 25

III. 51
III. 68
III. 72
IV. 119
V. 13
V. 40
VI. 2
VIII. 22

एषु **: eṣu**
इदम् (पुं)
III. 70

एष्यत् **: eṣyat**
इ
III. 13

ओजोनाशन **: ojonāśana**
IV. 85

ॐ **: Om**
ओम्
I. 1
VIII. 1

औघयोग **: aughayoga**
V. 37

औदारिक **: audārika**
I. 22

औदारिकसंग्रह **: audārikasaṁgr-aha**
IV. 66

औदार्य **: audārya**
II. 33

-औद्धत्य- **: –audhdatya–**
V. 48
V. 53

औद्धत्यमानमोह **: audhatyamāna-moha**
V. 45

औपचयिक **: aupacayika**
I. 37

औषध **: auṣadha**
VII. 53

औषधिः **: auṣadhiḥ**
III. 37

कः **: kaḥ**
किम्
II. 22

कण्ठोक्ति **: kaṇṭhokti**
(f)
III. 12

कण्ठगतप्राण **: kaṇṭāgatapraṇa**
VIII. 43

कथम् **: katham**
IV. 31
V. 27

कथा **: kathā**
(f)
I. 26

कथावस्तु **: kathāvastu**
(f)
I. 7

-कथिक **: –kathika**
–IV. 118
VIII. 40

-कर **: –kara**
–IV. 32

करूणा **: karuaṇā**
VIII. 29

करोटपाणय **: karotapanaya**
III. 64

काल : **kāla**
IV. 115

-काल- : **–kata–**
V. 25

-काल : **–kala**
IV. 35
VIII. 43

-कालतः : **–kālataḥ**
–V. 62

कालफलदिशुभतादिभिः : **kālaphalādiśub -hatadibhiḥ**
II. 51

काल्य : **kālya**
IV. 28

काव्य : **kāvya**
IV. 126

काश्मीर : **kāśmira**
IV. 39

काश्मीरवैभाषिकनीतिसिद्ध : **kāsmīravaibhāṣ-ikanītisiddha**
VIII. 40

काष्ट : **kāṣṭa**
II. 1

-काष्ठा- : **–kāṣṭhā–**
VII. 41

किम् : **kim**
किम् (नपुं)
V. 27

किल : **kil**
I. 3
I. 28
I. 42
II. 1
III. 25
IV. 27
IV. 31
V. 37

कीटाद्रिनवक : **kīṭādrīnavaka**
III. 57

-कीर्तन : **–kīrtana**
III. 25

कुकूल : **kukūla**
III. 59

कुक्षि : **kukṣi**
(f)
III. 18

कुक्षेत्र : **kukṣetra**
IV. 121

कुणप : **kuṇapa**
III. 59

कुतः : **kutaḥ**
IV. 108

कुतार्किक : **kutārkika**
VIII.41

कुप्रज्ञा : **kuprajñā**
(f)
III. 29

कुरव : **kurava**
III. 56

कुरू : **kuru**
III. 55
III. 78
IV. 43
IV. 82
IV. 84

कुरूतः : **kurutas**
कृ
II. 63

कुरूते : **kurute**
कृ
III. 24

कुरूबाहयोऽन्तरामृत्यु : **kurubāhyontar amṛtyu**
III. 85

कुर्यात् : **kuryāt**
कृ
VI. 14

कुर्वतः : **kurvataḥ**

कृ
IV.67

-कुर्वत्- : **–kurvat–**
IV. 4

कुर्वन् : **kurvan**
IV. 25

कुर्वन्त : **kurvanta**
IV. 23

कुलंकुल : **kulaṁkula**
VI. 34

कुलज : **kulaja**
IV. 108

कुशल : **kuśala**
II. 11
II. 25
II. 28
II. 54
II. 66
IV. 57
IV. 67
IV. 69
IV. 88
IV. 123
IV. 125
VII. 14

कुशलाकुशलेतरत् : **kuśalākuśaletar -at**

VII. 39
VII. 47
VII. 48
VII. 50
VII. 51
VII. 53^2
VII. 56
VIII. 7^2
VIII. 9^2
VIII. 10
VIII. 11^2
VIII. 13^2
VIII. 15
VIII. 16
VIII. 18^2
VIII. 21
VIII. 22
VIII. 23^2
VIII. 26
VIII. 30
VIII. 32
VIII. 38
VIII. 39
VIII. 41
VIII. 42
VIII. 43

-चक्र : –cakra
VI. 54^2

-चक्रक : –cakraka
III. 19

-चक्रभेद- : –cakrabheda–
IV. 101
IV. 102

-चक्रवर्ति- : -cakravarti -
III. 17

चक्रवर्तिसमुत्पत्ति : cakravartisamu tpatti
(f)
III. 95

चक्रवाड : carkavāḍa
III. 49

-चक्रिन् : –cakrin
III. 95

चक्षुस् : cakṣus
I. 19
I. 38
I. 41
I. 42
I. 43^2
I. 46^2
II. 18
IV. 75
VII. 44

-चक्षुस् : –cakṣu
VIII. 41

-चक्षु : –cakṣu
VII. 45

चक्षुरादय : cakṣurādaya
I. 9

चक्षुरादि : cakṣurādi
I. 45

चतस्र : catasra
(f)
III. 63
VII. 43

चतुर्गुण : caturguṇa
IV. 122

चतुर्दश : caturdaśa
I. 30
II. 6
VII. 49

चतुर्दशाकार : caturdaśakāra
VII. 12

चतुर्दिश : caturdiśa
III. 59
III. 68

चतुर्द्वीपक : caturdvipaka
III. 73

चतुर्धा : caturdhā
II. 72
III. 9
VI. 20
VI. 38
VII. 32
VIII. 17

चतुर् : catur
I. 15
I. 23
II. 1^2
II. 16
II. 18
II. 29
II. 61
II. 64
II. 67
II. 70
II. 71
II. 73
III. 7^2
III. 8
III. 34
III. 35
III. 63
III. 65
IV. 29
IV. 87
IV. 88
IV. 89
IV. 90
IV. 91
IV. 93^2
IV. 94
IV. 124
V. 5
V. 58
VI. 2
VI. 58

VII. 4
VII. 5
VII. 16
VII. 17
VII. 19
VIII. 1
VIII. 8
VIII. 29

-चतुर्- : –catur–
III.96

चतुरत्नमय : caturatnmaya
III. 50

चतुर्थ : caturtha
III. 2
III. 61
III. 101
VI. 42

चतुर्थक : caturthaka
VIII. 11

चतुर्थीयुक्तमुक्ताभिलापमार्गवशित्व : caturthīyuktam-uktābhilāpamār gavaśitva
VII. 38

चतुरस्र : caturaśra
III. 55

चतुराक्षेप : caturākṣepa
IV. 51

चतुरायतन : caturāyatana
VII. 49

चतुर्विंशति : caturviṁśati
III. 87

चतुर्विध : caturvidha
I. 10
II. 37
III. 3
IV. 14
IV. 59
IV. 74
V. 25
V. 61
VI. 34
VI. 65
VII. 4

-चतुर्विध- : –caturvidha–
V.34

चतुष्क : catuṣka
VI. 15
V. 9

चतुष्कोटि : catuṣkoṭi
III. 8

चतुष्कोटिक : catuṣkoṭika
IV. 51

चतुष्कोटिकसंभव : catuṣkoṭikasaṁ-bhava
VI. 79

चतुष्टय : catuṣṭaya
I. 36
VII. 10
VIII. 11

-चतुष्टय : –catuṣṭaya
III. 37
III. 87
VII. 43
VIII. 7

चतुष्फलव्यवस्था : catuṣphalavyav-asthā
(f)
VI. 52

चतुस् : catus
VIII. 36

चतुःसत्यगोचर : catuḥsatyagoca-ra
VI. 17

चतुःसार्धत्रिहस्तक : catuḥsārdhatrih-astaka
III. 75

चतुस्कन्ध : catuskandha
VIII. 2

चतुस्त्रिंशत् : catustriṁśat
II. 44

चत्वार्य : catvārya
V. 21

चर्यते : caryate
चर्
VIII. 42

चरम : carama
I. 44

चरित : carita
I. 26

-चरित : –carita
IV. 80
IV. 100

चन्द्र : candra
III. 73

चन्द्रार्क : candrārka
III. 60

-च्युत : –cyuta
III. 43
–VI. 38

च्युति : cyuti
(f)
III. 42

-च्युति : –cyuti
III. 43
IV. 38
VII. 42

-च्युति : –cyuti
VIII. 16

च्युतोद्भव : cyutodbhava

-चैतस् : **–caitas**
V. 46

चैतसी : **caitasī**
(f)
II. 7
II. 8
III. 32

चैतसिक : **caitasika**
II. 28

-चैत्ररथ : **–caitraratha**
III. 67

चैत्ररथपारूष्यमिश्रनन्दनभूषित : **caitrarathapāru-ṣyamiśranandan-bhūṣita**
III.67

चौर्यतः : **cauryataḥ**
IV. 73

छन्द : **chanda**
II. 24

-छित् : **–chit**
VI. 23

छिद्र : **chidra**
I. 28

छिद्यते : **chidyate**
I. 36

छिनत्ति : **chinatti**
√छिद्
I. 36
IV. 80

-छेद : **–cheda**
III. 44
IV. 38
IV. 41
IV. 42
IV. 79
IV. 111

छेदसंधान : **chedasandhāna**
III. 42

जगत् : **jagat**
I. 1
III. 38
VII. 34
VIII. 42

-जगत् : **–jagat**
I.1

जगौ : **jagau**
I. 25

-जन : **–jana**
VII. 35
VIII. 41

जनत्व : **janatva**
II. 40

जनिका : **janikā**
(f)
II. 46

-जन्म- : **–janma–**
IV. 95

जन्म : **janma**
VI. 36
VI. 41
VII. 42

जन्मनिश्रय : **janmaniśraya**
I. 28

-जन्मन् : **–janman**
IV. 118

-जन्मतस् : **–janmatas**
IV. 42

जन्य : **janya**
II. 46

जन्यन्ते : **janyante**
जन्
VIII. 31

जम्बूद्वीप : **jambnūdvīpa**
III. 53
IV. 101
IV. 109

-जय : **–jaya**
VI. 10
VII. 23

जरा : **jarā**
(f)
II. 45

जरामरण : **jarāmaraṇa**
III. 24

जरायुज : **jarāyuja**
III. 9

जल : **jala**
III. 50

जलकाञ्चनमण्डल : **jalakāñcanamaṇ-ḍala**
III. 47

जहाति : **jahāti**
हा
V. 70
VI. 79

जात : **jāta**
IV. 5

-जातवत् : **–jātavat**
VI. 47

जाति : **jāti**
(f)
I. 19
II. 45
II. 46
III. 24
VII. 34

जातिस्मर : **jātismara**
IV. 108

जात्यादि : **jātyādi**
II. 46

नते : jānate
VII. 56

म्बूद्वीप : jāṁbūdvipa
III. 75

यते : jāyate
न्
II. 58
IV. 102

यन्ते : jāyante
न्
II. 64
III. 27

यमान : jāyamāna
II. 63

यमानसशैक्ष : jāyamānasasakṣa
VI. 77

ता : jitā
(f)
VII. 52

हा : jihvā
I. 30

ीव : –jīva
IV. 27
IV. 86

वित : jīvita
II. 3
II. 9
II. 10
II. 15

-जीवित- : –jivita–
II. 35
II. 45

-जीवित : –jivita
II.17
II.20
III. 3

तण्डुलवत् : taṇḍulvat
III. 37

तदा : tada
II.37

तत् (तद् पुं) : tat
I. 2

तद् : tad
I. 3
I. 9
I. 16
I. 17
I. 39
I. 42

तत् : tat
II. 10
II. 14
II. 30
II. 40
II. 58
II.63
II. 65[2]
II. 67

तद् तद् (नपुं) : tad
II. 68

तत् (नपुं) : tat
II. 70[2]
III. 6
III. 22
III. 24
III. 29

तद् तद् (पुं) : tad
III. 56

तत् : tat
III. 58
III. 67
III. 74[2]

तद् (तद् - नपुं) : tad
III. 93

तद् (तद् - पुं) : tad
III. 94
III 101[2]

तत् : tat
IV 1[2]
IV. 3

तद् : tad
IV. 46

तत् : tat
IV. 50
IV. 53
IV. 54

तद् : tad
IV. 55

तत् : tat
IV. 61

तद् : tad
IV. 66
IV. 75
IV. 99

तत् : tat
IV. 109

तद् : tad
IV. 112
IV. 113[2]
IV. 114
IV. 122
IV. 123
V. 7
V. 9
V. 15

तत् : **tat**
V. 27

तद् : **tad**
V. 28
V. 52

तत् : **tat**
V. 67

तद् : **tad**
VI. 3
VI. 4^2
VI. 7

तत् : **tat**
VI. 17

तद् : **tad**
VI. 39

तत् : **tat**
VI. 43
VI. 45

तद् : **tad**
तद् (नपुं)
VI. 54
VI. 60
V.72

तत् : **tat**
VII. 15
VII.1
VII.5
VII.9

तद् : **tad**
VII. 22

तत् : **tat**
VII. 31
VII. 37
VII. 41

तद् : **tad**
VII. 46^2

तत् : **tat**
VII. 50^2
VII. 56
VIII. 1
VIII. 6^2
VIII. 13^2
VIII. 17
VIII. 23^2
VII.40

-तद्- : **–tad–**
(तद् नपुं)
III. 86

-तत्- : **–tat–**
IV. 10

-तद्- : **–tad–**
IV. 123

-तत्- : **–tat–**
VI. 74

ततः : **tataḥ**
II. 63
III. 27^2
III. 49
III. 57
III. 69
III. 72^2
III. 76
III. 91
III. 97
III. 98
III. 102
IV. 116
V. 32
V. 33^2
V. 52
VI. 17
VI. 26
VII. 50
VIII. 33

तत्काल : **tatkāla**
VI. 8

तत्कृत : **tatkṛta**
IV. 1

तत्क्षण : **tatkṣaṇa**
III. 88

तत्क्षय : **tatkṣaya**
IV. 60

तत्ज : **tatja**
IV. 1

तत्जा : **tatjā**
(f)
III. 32

-तत्व : **–tatva**
VIII. 41

तत्पक्ष्य : **tatpakṣya**
VI.6

तत्पथ : **tatpatha**
IV. 24

तत्पालन : **tatpālana**
IV. 31

तत्लाभिन् : **tatlābhin**
VII. 40

तत्संचर : **tatsañcara**
VII. 25

तत्र : **tatra**
I. 5
III. 2
III. 8
III. 45
III. 48
III. 53
IV. 52
V. 51
VI. 9
VI. 22

II. 53
II. 63
II. 64
II. 65
II. 70
III. 2
III. 8
III. 18
III. 21
III. 23
III. 25
III. 30
III. 34
III. 36
III. 44
III. 48
III. 52
III. 53
III. 54
III. 61
III. 74
III. 75
III. 76
III. 77
III. 78
III. 79
III. 80
IV. 2
IV. 3
IV. 11
IV. 12

IV. 14
IV. 18
IV. 20
IV. 23
IV. 30^2
IV. 36^2
IV. 37
IV. 39
IV. 40
IV. 41
IV. 42
IV. 47
IV. 57
IV. 63
IV. 65
IV. 68^2
IV. 71
IV. 77
IV. 79
IV. 83
IV. 91
IV. 93
IV. 94
IV. 97
IV. 98
IV. 122
IV. 123
IV. 127
V. 6
V. 9
V. 18

V. 19
V. 24
V. 37
V. 38
V. 43
V. 46
V. 51
V. 55
V. 57
V. 67
VI. 1
VI. 15
VI. 18
VI. 19^2
VI. 20
VI. 21
VI. 31
VI. 34
VI. 35
VI. 49
VI. 52
VI. 53
VI. 54
VI. 59
VI. 61
VI. 63
VI. 66
VI. 67
VI. 69
VI. 75

VI. 76
VI. 77
VI. 78
VIII. 3
VII. 9
VII. 13
VII. 14
VII. 15
VII. 19
VII. 22
VII. 25
VII. 27
VII. 28
VII. 29
VII. 32
VII. 37
VII. 39
VII. 44
VII. 46
VII. 49
VII. 51
VII. 52^2
VII. 53
VII. 56
VIII. 1
VIII. 3
VIII. 4
VIII. 8
VIII. 9
VIII. 11
VIII. 14

VIII. 16^2
VIII. 20
VIII. 25
VIII. 26
VIII. 30
VIII. 31
VIII. 33
VIII. 34
VIII. 37
VIII. 38

तुलयति : **tulayati**
√(तुल्)
I. 36

तुल्य : **tulya**
I. 36
III. 82
IV. 12

तुल्यविषयग्रहण : **tuluviṣayagrah-aṇa**
I. 44

तुषवत् : **tuṣavat**
III. 36

तुषिन् : **tuṣin**
III. 37

तुष्टयात्मक : **tuṣṭyâtmaka**
VI. 7

तृतीय : **tṛtīya**
II. 7
V. 26
VIII. 8
VIII. 15
VIII. 32

-तृतीयगा : **–tṛtīyagā**
VIII. 19

तृतीयप्रतिपन्नक : **tṛtīyapratipann-aka**
VI. 30
VI. 36

तृतीया : **tṛtīyā**
(f)
VII. 44
VII. 47

तृष्णा : **tṛṣṇā**
(f)
III. 23
V. 20

तृष्णादृड्.मानमोह : **tṛṣṇādṛñmāna-moha**
V. 21

तृष्णांतपादविपक्षतः : **tṛṣṇantpādavip a- kṣataḥ**
VI. 8

ते : **te**
(तद् पुं)
I. 7^2
I. 8^2
I. 14
I. 29
I. 34
II. 32
II. 41
II. 46
II. 55
III. 51
III. 88^2
III. 92
III. 93
III. 95
IV. 2
IV. 14
IV. 67
IV. 94
V. 1
V. 5
V. 13
V. 21
V. 23
V. 26
V. 36
V. 41
V. 46^2
V. 64
VI. 17
VI. 69
VII. 4^2
VII. 6
VII. 50
VIII. 25
VIII. 34

तेज : **teja**
I.12
I. 13

तेजस् : **tejas**
III. 102

तेन : **tena**
तद् (नपुं)
III. 39
III. 79
IV. 98
IV. 99

तेभ्यः : **tebhayaḥ**
तद् (पुं)
VI. 18

तेषाम् : **teṣām**
तद् (नपुं)
II. 46
II. 51
III. 59
III. 82
V. 63
VI. 7
VI. 56

तेषु : **teṣu**
तद् (पुं)

I. 4
III. 4
IV. 56
VI. 29

तैः : taiḥ
तद् (पुं)
I. 44
I. 45
IV. 29
III. 82
VIII. 31

तौ : tau
तद् (पुं)
I. 33
II. 60
IV. 18
IV. 21
VI. 7
VI. 13
VI. 31

त्यक्त : tyakta
IV. 25
VI. 46

त्यक्त्वा : tyaktvā
VI. 62

त्यजति : tyajati
√त्यज्
VI. 21

त्यज्यते : tyajyate
√त्यज्
IV. 40

-त्याग : –tyāga
VI. 10
VI. 21
VI. 52

त्यागान्वय : tyāgānvaya
IV. 121

त्रय : traya
IV. 83
V. 43
V. 66
VI. 7

-त्रय- : –traya–
V. 29
V. 30^2
V. 31
VIII. 25

-त्रय : –traya
II. 13
III. 100
IV. 32
IV. 64^2
IV. 96
IV. 45

-त्रय : –traya
V. 53
VI. 26
VI. 63
VI. 74
VII. 20
VIII. 25

त्रया : trayā
V. 9

त्रयाप्ति : trayāpti
(f)
VI. 55

त्रयोदश : trayodaśa
II. 19

त्रयोद्भव : trayodbhava
III. 93

-त्रिंशत् : –triṁśat
VI. 67

त्रिंशद्गुणोत्तर : triṁśadguṇottara
III. 88

त्रि (पुं) : tri
I. 15
I. 31
I. 32
I. 38
I. 40
I. 43
I. 44
I. 47
II. 9^2
II. 13
II. 17
II. 63
II. 64
II. 69
II. 71
II. 73
III. 26
III. 31
III. 33
III. 38
III. 40
III. 47
III. 89
III. 100
IV. 29
IV. 43
IV. 45
IV. 48
IV. 51
IV. 65
IV. 71
IV. 75
IV. 78
IV. 82
IV. 88^2
IV. 89^3

IV. 90
IV. 91^2
IV. 92
IV. 93^2
IV. 97
IV. 101
IV. 110
IV. 112
V. 10
V. 20
V. 43
V. 52
VI. 8
VI. 23
VI. 24
VI. 25
VI. 39
VI. 55
VI. 72
VII. 16
VII. 19
VII. 32
VII. 44

-त्रि : **–tri**
III.54
VIII. 18^2

-त्रि- : **tri–**
III.96
VII.55

त्रिक : **trika**
III. 22

त्रिकाण्डक : **trikāṇḍaka**
III. 20

त्रिगुण : **triguṇa**
III. 48
III. 52

त्रिचतुर्विधमुक्त : **tricaturvidham-ukta**
VI. 34

त्रिदुःखतायोग : **tridukhatāyoga**
VI. 3

त्रिदेशना : **trideśanā**
V. 44

त्रिद्विदृष्टिविवर्जित : **tridvidṛṣṭivivarj-ita**
V. 4

त्रिधा : **tridhā**
I. 30
I. 38
I. 40
II. 38
II. 39
II. 65
III. 38
IV. 7
IV. 12
IV. 13
IV. 51
IV. 64
IV. 65
IV. 125
IV. 126
VI. 27
VI. 59^2
VII. 14
VII. 48
VIII. 5
VIII. 22
VIII. 23

त्रिधातु : **tridhātu**
V. 30

-त्रिधातु- : **–tridhātu–**
V. 31
VI. 7

त्रिधातुप्रतिपक्ष : **tridhātupratipa-kṣa**
VII. 9

त्रिधात्वाश्रय : **tridhātvāśraya**
VIII. 37

-त्रिध्यान- : **–tridhyāna–**
III. 71

-त्रिपार्श्व : **–tripārśva**
III. 53

त्रिप्रकार : **triprakāra**
I. 32

त्रिभुजा : **tribhujā** (f)
VI. 48

त्रिभूमिक : **tribhūmika**
III. 2

त्रिमूलज : **trimūlaja**
IV. 68

त्रिमूलजा : **trimūlajā**
IV. 69

त्रियोजन : **triyojana**
III. 54
III. 77

त्रिविध : **trividha**
I. 5
II. 37
IV. 50
VI. 39
VII. 53

त्रिविधामलरूपोक्तिवृ-द्धयकुर्वत्पथादि : **trividhāmalaru-poktivṛddhyak-urvatpathādi**
IV. 4

त्रिशतयोजन : **triśatayojana**
III. 54

त्रिसत्यदर्शन : **trisatyadarśana**
VI. 73

ासाहस्त्र : **trisāhasra**
III. 74

त्रिहस्तक : **–trihastak**
III. 75

धा : **tredhā**
II. 11
II. 13
VII. 56

ध : **traidha**
I. 20

धातुक : **traidhātuka**
II. 73
VII. 18

धातुकाश्रय : **traidhātukāśra ya**
VII. 15

यध्विक : **traiyadhvika**
II. 37

यन्वित : **tryanvita**
VIII. 31

यायतनात्मक : **tryāyatanātma ka**
III. 39

क् : **dak**
VII. 1

क्षिणा : **dakṣiṇā**
IV. 118

दक्षिणावर : **dakṣiṇāvara**
III. 68

दक्षिणोत्तरग : **dakṣiṇottaraga**
III. 62

दग्धृ : **dagdhṛ**
I. 36

ददत : **dadata**
√दा
IV. 111

ददाति : **dadāti**
√दा
IV. 115

दर्शन : **darśana**
III. 29
III. 72
VI. 58
VI. 70
VII. 20
VIII. 28

-दर्शन- : **–darśana–**
IV. 56
VI. 1

-दर्शन : **–darśana**
I. 43
V. 4
V. 19
VI. 73

दर्शनक्षण : **darśanakṣaṇa**
VII. 6

दर्शनस्थ : **darśanastha**
V. 69

दर्शनाख्य : **darśanākhya**
VI. 1

दर्शनालम्बकार्याख्य : **darśanālambak -āryākhya**
VI. 27

दश : **daśa**
I. 29
I. 35
I. 40
II. 10
II. 15
II. 22
II. 67
III. 21
IV. 15
IV. 66
IV. 81
IV. 83
V. 4
VI. 67
VII. 8
VII. 17
VII. 25
VII. 28
VII. 29[2]
VII. 39
VIII. 9
VIII. 36

-दश : **–daśa**
V. 3
VI. 28

दशभू : **daśabhū**
VI. 11

दशम : **daśama**
VII. 32

दशवर्षायुस् : **daśavarṣāyus**
III. 91

दशवर्षोपम : **daśavarṣopama**
III. 70

दशाधिक : **daśādhika**
VII. 31

दशाब्द : **daśābda**
III. 78

दशायतनधातु : **daśāyatanadhātu**
I. 14

दशायुष् : **daśāyuṣa**
III. 98

दशैक : **daśaika**
II. 68

दशसाहस्रिकान्तर : **daśasāhasrikānt-ara**
III. 63

दहयते : **dhayate**
√दह्
I. 36

दातृ : **dātṛ**
IV. 115

दातृवस्तुक्षेत्रविशेषत : **dātṛvastukṣetra -viseṣeata**
IV. 114

दान : **dāna**
IV. 113

-दान : **–dāna**
IV. 125

दानपूरण : **dānapūraṇa**
IV. 111

-दिक् : **–dik**
III. 65

दिवस : **divasa**
III. 99

दिवौकस् : **divoukas**
III. 1
III. 76
III. 79

-दिवौकस् : **–divoukas**
III. 73

दिव्यश्रोत्राक्षिन् : **divyaśrotrākṣin**
VII. 54

-दिव्याक्षि- : **–divyākṣi–**
III. 14

दीपकृत् : **dīpakṛt**
IV. 110

दीयते : **dīyate**
√दा
IV. 113
IV. 114

दुःख : **dukhha**
I. 8
II. 7
II. 9
II. 12
VI. 2
VI. 3
VI. 26
VI. 66

-दुःख- : **–dukha–**
IV. 117
V. 55
VI. 19
VII. 3^2
VIII. 34

-दुःख : **–dukha**
VI. 26

-दुःखतः : **–dukhataḥ**
VI. 16

दुःखता : **dukhatā**
(f)
VI. 3

दुःखदृग्घेय : **dukhuadṛgheya**
V. 8
V. 28

दुःखन : **dukhana**
IV. 85

दुःखवेघ : **dukhavedya**
IV. 47

दुःशोधत्व : **duḥśodhatva**
IV. 86

दुःखहेतुक्षान्तिज्ञान : **dukhahetukṣānt -ijñāna**
VI. 79

दुःखहेतुदृग्भ्यासप्रहेय : **dukhahetudṛga -bhyāsapraheya**
V. 29

दुःखहेतुदृग्घेया : **dukhahetudṛgh -eyā**
V. 12

दुःखहेतुधीः : **dukhahetudhīḥ**
VII. 17

दुःखहेत्वन्वयज्ञान : **dukhahetvanva -yajñāna**
VII. 5

-दुःखादि : **–dukhādi**
III. 22

दुःखादिदर्शन : **dukhādidarśana**
V. 4

दुःखिता : **dukhitā**
(f)
VIII. 30

दुःखिन् : **dukhin**
II. 18

दुर्गति : **durgati**
IV. 96

-दुर्गृहीत : **–durgṛhīta**
VIII. 40

दुर्भिक्ष : **durbhikṣa**
III. 99

दुर्मनस्क : **durmanaska**
II. 13

दुचरित : **duścarita**
IV. 24
IV. 65^2

दूर : **dūra**
I. 23

दूरता : **dūratā**
(f)
V. 62

दूषण : **dūṣaṇa**
IV. 106

दूषणाख्य : **dūṣaṇākhya**
V. 61

दूरसूक्ष्मादिगोचर : **dūrasūkṣmādig -ocara**
VII. 54

-दृक्- : **–dṛk–**
V. 8
V. 12
V. 14^2
V. 21
V. 28
V. 29
V. 31

-दृक् : **–drk**
VI. 22

दृक्त : **dṛktaḥ**
V. 32

दृक्चरित : **dṛkcarita**
IV. 100

दृक्पथ : **dṛkpatha**
VI. 55

दृग्घेय : **dṛggheya**
IV. 63
IV. 93
V. 6

दृङ्मात्र : **–dṛṅgmātra**
VI. 28

दृङ्मार्ग : **dṛṅmārga**
VI. 54

दृग्भावना : **dṛugbhāvana**
(f)
II. 9
V. 6

दृग्भावनाक्षय : **dṛgbhāvanākṣaya**
V. 10

दृश : **dṛśa**
V. 33
VII. 1

दृश- : **–drsa–**
VII. 55

दृग्हेया : **drgheyā**
V. 54

दृष्टधर्मफल : **dṛṣṭadharmafala**
IV. 53
IV. 55

दृष्टधर्मादिवेद्यत्व : **drstadharmādi-vedyatva**
IV. 50

दृष्टश्रुतविज्ञात : **drstaśrutavijña ta**
IV. 75

दृष्टयामर्श : **drsṭuāmarśa**
V. 51

-दृश्य : **–dṛśya**
VI. 11
VIII. 34

-दृश्य : **– dṛśya**
III. 14
VII. 55

दृश्यते : **dṛśyate**

दृश्
I. 42

दृष्टि : **drsti**
(f)
I. 41^2
III. 29
IV. 78
IV. 80
V. 1
V. 3
V. 7^2
V. 12
V. 37
V. 41
VI. 50
VI. 61

-दृष्टि- : **–drsti–**
V. 4
V. 55

दृष्टिचरित : **drsticarita**
IV. 80

दृष्टित्रयाद्विपर्यासचतुष्क : **drstitrayādvipr-yāsacatuṣka**
V. 9

दृष्टिद्वयविवर्जित : **drstidvagavivar-jita**
V. 13

दृष्टिपुष्टत्व : **drstipuṣṭatva**
V. 11

दृष्टिप्राप्तान्वय : **drstiprāptānvaya**
VI. 57

दृष्टियुक्त : **drstiyukta**
II. 29

दृष्टिविवेचन : **drstivivecana**
V. 38

दृष्टिशीलव्रतपरामर्श : **drstiśilavratapa-rāmarśa**
V. 3

दृष्टिसमुत्थित : **drstisamutthita**
V. 51

दृष्टिस्थान : **drstisthāna**
I. 8

दृष्टिहेय : **drstiheya**
I. 40
IV. 11

देव : **devā**
III. 9
III. 69
IV. 43

-देव : **–deva**
III. 64
IV. 44

-देश- : **–deśa–**
V. 62
I. 35
III. 15

-देशना : **–deśanā**
IV. 125

देशस्थ : **deśaṣtha**
III. 97

देह : **deha**
III. 56

-दैशिक : –daiśika
VII. 55

दोष : doṣa
VI. 33

-दोष- : –doṣa–
IV. 59
VI. 36

दौःशील्य : dauśīlya
IV. 24
IV. 122

दौःशील्यतद्धेत्वहत : dauḥśīlyatadhet-vahata
IV. 123

दौर्मनस्य : daurmansya
II. 8
II. 10
II. 11
V. 56
V. 57

-द्रव्य- : –dravya–
II. 22

-द्रव्य : –dravya
II. 22[2]
VIII. 5

द्रव्यगोचर : dravyagocara
VII. 11

द्रव्यतस् : dravyatas
IV. 14

द्रव्यतः : dravyataḥ
VI. 67
VI. 75
VII. 13
VIII. 9

द्रव्यामर्शनसामान्य : dravyāmarśana-sāmānya
V. 41

द्रव्यवान् : dravyavān
I. 38

द्वंद्व : dvandva
III. 69

द्वंद्वालिंड.गगूनपाण्याप्तिवसितेक्षितमैथुन : dvandvāliṅgana-pāṇyaptivasitek-ṣitamaithuna
III. 69

द्वय : dvaya
VIII. 35

-द्वय- : –dvaya–
V. 13
V. 64
V. 68

-द्वय : –dvaya
V. 42

द्वयध्वग : dvyadhvaga
II. 55

द्वयवर्जित : dvayavarjita
VI. 72

-द्वयवत् : –dvayavat
VI. 6

-द्वयान : –dvayāna
V. 62

द्वयाश्रय : dvyāśraya
VI. 21

द्वयेकता (f) : dvyekatā
V. 59

द्वयोदय : dvayodaya
III. 12

द्वादश : dvādaśa
I. 39
I. 48
II. 10
II. 30
II. 71
III. 33

द्वादशगोचर : dvādaśagocara
III. 33

द्वादशधा : dvādaśadhā
IV. 61

द्वादशमासक : dvādaśamāsaka
III. 89

द्वादशाङ.गृ : dvādaśaṅgah
III. 20

द्वार : dvāra
I. 20

-द्वार- : –dvara–
IV. 106

द्वाविंशति : dvāviṁśati
II. 28

द्वाविंशतिविध : dvāviṁśatividha
IV. 53

द्वि (पुं) : dvi
I. 5
I. 19
II. 1
II.14
II.16
II. 21
II. 51
II. 56
II. 59[2]
II. 63
II. 64[2]
II. 73
III. 12
III. 26[2]
III. 34
III. 41[2]
III. 43
III. 53
III. 55
III. 63

III. 78
III. 94
IV. 18
IV. 39
IV. 63
IV. 88
IV. 89[2]
IV. 90
IV. 91
IV. 92[3]
IV. 93
IV. 94
V. 25
V. 43
V. 45
V. 64[2]
V. 67
V. 69
V. 70
VI. 20
VI. 22[2]
VI. 23
VI. 62
VI. 63[2]
VI. 65
VI. 72[2]
VI. 75
VI. 76
VII. 17
VII. 29
VII. 46
VII. 49
VII. 50
VIII. 18
VIII. 26
VIII. 32
VIII. 35
VIII. 36
VIII. 38

-द्वि- : –dvi–
V. 4
V. 9

III. 66
III. 96[2]

द्विकाल : dvikāla
IV. 21

द्विगुणद्विगुणा : dviguṇadviguṇā
III. 77

-द्विगुणा : –dviguṇā
III. 77

द्विगुणोत्तर : dviguṇottara
III. 80

द्विगुणोत्तरवृद्धि : dviguṇottarvṛd-dhi
III. 75

द्विग्राहय : dvigrāhya
IV. 3

द्वितीय : dvitīya
III. 61
IV. 10
VI. 30
VI. 72
VII. 19
VIII. 7

द्वितीयप्रतिपन्नक : dvitīyapratipan-naka
VI. 35

द्वितीयवत् : dvitīyavat
VIII. 35

द्वितीयसप्तम : dvitīyasaptama
VII. 32

द्वितीयादि : dvitīyādi
III. 100
VIII. 13

द्वित्व : dvitva
I. 19

द्वित्रिजन्मन् : dvitrijanman
VI. 34

द्वित्रिसाहस्रक : dvitrisāhasraka
VII. 55

द्विधा : dvidhā
I. 10
I. 34
II. 9
II. 10
II. 11
II. 38
II. 48
II. 65
II. 66
II. 71
IV. 10
IV. 67
IV. 82
IV. 122[2]
V. 32
V. 38
V. 39
V. 51
V. 52
VI. 18
VI. 45
VI. 46
VI. 71
VI. 75
VII. 2
VII. 18
VII. 49
VIII. 1
VIII. 5
VIII. 18

-द्विधा- : –dvidha–
IV. 43

द्विधागम : dvidhāgama
VIII. 9

द्विधातुज : dvidhātuja
V. 2

द्विपक्षतः : dvipakṣataḥ

V. 18

-द्विपक्षत्व- : **–dvipakṣatva–**
V. 62

द्विलक्षणपरीक्षण : **dvilakṣaṇapakī-kṣaṇa**
VI. 14

द्विलिड.ग् : **dviliṅga**
II. 21

द्विविज्ञेय : **dvivijñeya**
I. 48

द्विविध : **dvividha**
I. 35
IV. 67
VI. 1
VIII. 39

द्विवेद्या : **dvivedyā**
(f)
II. 43

-द्विव्यञ्जन- : **–dvivyañjana–**
IV. 41

-द्विशत- : **–dviśata–**
III. 67

द्विसाहस्र : **dvisāhasra**
III. 74

द्विसाहस्रस्त्रिपार्श्व : **dvisāhasrastrip-arśva**
III. 53

द्विहेया : **dviheyā**
(f)
II. 13

द्वीप : **dvipa**
III. 49
IV. 97
IV. 101

-द्वीप- : **–dvipa–**
III.1
III.56

-द्वीपक : **–dvipka**
III. 73

-द्वीपा : **–dvīpā**
III. 96

द्वे (नपुं) : **dve**
III. 20^2

द्वेधा : **dvedhā**
II. 10

द्वेष : **dveṣa**
IV. 70
V. 16
V. 33
V. 55

-द्वेष- : **–dvesa–**
IV. 69

-द्वेषज- : **–dveṣaja–**
IV. 59

द्वैध : **dvaidha**
V. 21

धनर्णवत् : **dhanarṇavat**
IV. 39

धनुस् : **dhanus**
III. 87

धन्याभिज्ञा : **dhanyābhijñā**
(f)
VI. 66

धर्म : **dharma**
I. 3
I. 4
I. 7
I. 30
I. 35
I. 48
II. 57
IV. 32
IV. 92
IV. 98
IV. 127
VI. 18^2
VI. 74
VII. 17
VII. 18
VII. 35
VII. 40

-धर्म- : **–dharma–**
I. 1
I. 2
II. 46
IV. 50
IV. 53
IV. 55
VI. 29
VI. 73
VII. 34

-धर्मा : **–dharmā**
(f)
IV. 91
VI. 19

-धर्म : **–dharma**
I. 2

-धर्मक : **–dharmaka**
VII. 21

-धर्मकोश : **–dharmakośa**
I. 1

धर्मक्षान्ति : **dharmakṣānti**
IV. 61

धर्मक्षान्तिरनास्रवा : **dharmakṣāntir-nāsravā**
(f)
VI. 25

धर्मचक्र : **dharmacakra**
VI. 54

धर्मज्ञान : **dharmajñāna**
V. 67
VI. 26
VII. 2

धर्मज्ञाननिरोध : **dharmajñānani**

I. 28

धात्वाख्या : **dhātvākhyā** (f)
VI. 78

धात्वोरारूप्योत्पादन : **dhātvorārupyot-pādana**
VIII. 38

-धामकथिक : **–dhāmakathika**
IV. 118

-धारण : **–dhāraṇa**
VI. 11

धीः : **dhīḥ**
I. 41
II. 57
VI. 4
VI. 5
VII. 1
VII. 16

-धी- : **–dhī–**
VII. 6
VII. 16

धी : **dhī**
VII. 1
VII. 16
VII. 16
VII. 17

VII. 33
VII. 42

धीभेद : **dhībheda**
VIII. 28

धीसमाधी : **dhīsamādhī**
IV. 112

ध्रुव : **dhrūva**
IV. 9
VIII. 31

-ध्रुव- : **–dhruva–**
V. 7

धृति : **dṛti**
VI. 53

धृत्यादिकर्मसंसिद्ध : **dhṛtyādikarma-saṁsiddha**
I. 12.

-धूर्धर : **–dhūrdhara**
VIII. 42

ध्यान : **dhyāna**
II. 7
II. 31
II. 42
III. 2
V. 66
VI. 24
VI. 37
VI. 48
VI. 66
VI. 71
VII. 15
VII. 29
VII. 36
VIII. 1
VIII. 20
VIII. 22
VIII. 27
VIII. 28
VIII. 31
VIII. 32
VIII. 36
VIII. 38

-ध्यान- : **–dhyana–**
VI. 20
VII. 53

-ध्यान- : **–dhyana–**
VII. 30
VII. 40

ध्यानचतुष्टय : **dhyānacatuṣṭaya**
VII. 43

ध्यानज : **dhyānaja**
IV. 13
IV. 17
IV. 26
IV. 44

ध्यानत्रय : **dhyānatraya**
III. 100

ध्यानादातृतीया : **dhyānādātṛtīyā**
IV. 47

ध्यानद्वय : **dhyānadvaya**
III. 33
III. 34

ध्यानफल : **dhyānaphala**
VII. 50

ध्यानभूमि : **dhyānabhūmi**
IV. 26

ध्यानभूमिक : **dhyānabhūmika**
VII. 54

ध्यानानास्रव : **dhyānānāsrava**
IV. 35

ध्यानान्तर : **dhyānāntara**
II. 31
VI. 72

ध्यानान्तरविपाकत : **dhyānāntaravip-ākatas**
IV. 48

ध्यानान्तरासंज्ञिसत्ववर्ज्य : **dhyānāntarasaṅ-jñisattvavarjya**
IV.44

ध्यानारूप्य : **dhyānārupya**

VI. 1
VII. 1
VIII. 1

नमस्कृत्य : **namaskṛtya**
I. 1

नय : **naya**
III. 27

नर : **nara**
III. 9

नरक : **naraka**
III. 1^2
III. 58
III. .90
IV. 51
IV. 82

नरकादि : **narakādi**
III. 4

नरकासंभव : **narakāsaṁbhava**
III. 90

नरकद्वीपभेद : **narakadvipabh-eda**
III. 1

नरकप्रेततिर्यञ्च : **narakpretatiry-añca**
III. 1

नरकवेद्य : **narakavedya**
IV. 63

नव : **nava**
I. 34^2
I. 35
II. 9^2
II. 13
II. 15
II. 67
II. 68
II. 70
III. 6
V. 13
V. 64
VI. 39
VI. 60
VI. 61
VI. 62
VII. 14
VII. 16
VII. 17
VII. 25
VII. 28
VII. 39

-नव- : **–nava–**
V. 15

-नव : **–nava**
II. 16

नवादि : **navādi**
IV. 101

नवाप्ति : **navāpti**
(f)
II. 16

-नवक : **–navaka**
III. 57

नवक्षय : **navakṣaya**
VI. 30
VI. 36

नवति : **navati**
VI. 51

-नवति : **–navti**
V. 5

नवत्रिध्यानभूमि : **navatridhyanb-hūmi**
(f)
III. 71

नवद्रव्य : **navadravya**
II. 22

नवधा : **navadhā**
VI. 62

नवप्रकार : **navaprakāra**
VI. 33

नवभूमि : **navabhūmi**
(f)
II. 52

नवम : **navam**
IV. 62
VI. 44

-नवमी : **–navamī**
III. 61

नवविधा : **navavidhā**
V. 10

-नष्टता : **–naṣṭatā**
V. 27

नष्टाजात : **naṣṭājāta**
VII. 5

नागवत् : **nāgavat**
III. 36

-नाटयवत् : **–nāṭyavat**
IV. 77

नानाकरण : **nānākaraṇa**
VII. 33

नानात्वकायसंज्ञा : **nānātvakāyasa-ṁjñā**
III. 5

नानाकायैकसंज्ञिन् : **nānākāyaiksaṁ-jñin**
III. 5

नानास्रव : **nānāsrava**
V. 18

नाभि : **nābhi**
(f)
III. 15

-नाभि- : **–nabhi–**

III. 43

म : **nāma**
III. 30
III. 66
IV. 71
VII. 38

ाम- : **–nāma–**
III. 4

मकाय : **nāmakāya**
II. 36

मकायादि : **nāmakāyadi**
II. 47

मतः : **nāmataḥ**
VI. 67

मरूप : **nāmarūpa**
IV. 71

मरूपतः : **nāmarūpataḥ**
III. 21

मसञ्चार : **nāmasañcāra**
IV. 14

मोभयार्थविषया : **nāmobhayārtha-viṣayā** (f)
VI. 5

रक : **nāraka**
III. 9
III. 15
VII. 56

नारायणबल : **nārāyaṇabala**
VII. 31

-नाश : **–nāśa**
IV. 29

-नाशन : **–nāśana**
IV. 85

निकाय : **nikāya**
II. 3
III. 3
IV. 53

-निकाय- : **–nikaya–**
II. 52

निकायाक्षेपण : **nikāyākṣepaṇa**
IV. 51

-निक्षेपण : **–nikṣepaṇa**
IV. 38

नितीरण : **nitīraṇa**
V. 9

नित्य : **nitya**
I. 48
III. 16
III. 101
IV. 19
VII. 54

नित्यात्मविपर्यास : **nityātmavipary-āsa**
V. 8

निर्भूषण : **nirbhūṣaṇa**
IV. 28

निमित्त : **nimitta**
I. 14

निमिन्धरगिरि : **nimindharagiri**
III. 49

निमीलित : **nimīlita**
VIII. 41

नियत : **niyata**
IV. 50
IV. 54
IV. 55

-नियत : **–niyata**
III. 44

नियतानियत : **niyatāniyata**
IV. 50

नियतिस्थ : **nigatistha**
IV. 106

निर्गम : **nirgama**
III. 99

निरङ्‌कुश : **niraṁkuśa**
VIII. 42

निर्मल : **nirmala**
VI. 75
VII. 11
VIII. 25

निर्माण : **nirmāṇa**
VII. 48
VII. 51

निर्माणचित्त : **nirmāṇacitta**
VII. 49

निर्मातृ : **nirmātṛ**
VII. 51

निर्मित : **nirmita**
VII. 49

निरवग्रह : **niravagraha**
VIII. 41

-निराकृति- : **–nirākṛti–**
IV. 103

निरास्रव : **nirāsrava**
IV. 60

निरूक्त : **nirukta**
VII. 37

निरूक्ति : **nirukti** (f)
V. 40

निरूच्यते (नि + वच्) : **niruchyate**
I. 45

निरूध्यमान : **nirudhyamāna**
II. 63
VI. 77

निरूपण : **nirupaṇa**
I. 33

निरोध : **nirodha**
I. 5
I. 6
II. 36
II. 41

VI. 52

पञ्चता : **pañcatā**
(f)
V. 59

पञ्चदश : **pañcadaśā**
VI. 28

पञ्चधा : **pañcadhā**
II. 23
II. 34
IV. 49
IV. 50
V. 41
V. 43
V. 45
VII. 53

पञ्चप्रकारघ्न : **pañcaprakārag-hna**
VI. 30

पञ्चभू : **pañcabhū**
VI. 12

पञ्चम : **pañcama**
IV. 107

पञ्चवर्षशतम् : **pañcavarṣaśatam**
III. 79

पञ्चवर्षोपम : **pañcavarṣopama**
III. 70

पञ्चविज्ञानसहज : **pañcavijñānasa-haja**
I. 41

पञ्चशत : **pancaśata**
III. 87

पञ्चाशत् : **pañcāśat**
III. 57
III. 60
III. 79

पञ्चस्कन्धा : **pañcaskandhā**
(f)
VI. 19
VIII. 1

पञ्चोन्द्रिय : **pañcendriya**
I. 9

पञ्चोक्ति : **pañcokti**
(f)
III. 12

-पण्ड- : **–paṇḍa–**
IV. 43

पतनीय : **pataniya**
IV. 39

पतित : **patita**
II. 36

-पत्रप : **–patrapa**
V. 48

पथ : **patha**
VII.23

-पथ- : **–patha–**
III. 98
IV. 4
IV. 61

-पथ- : **:–patha**
II.9
IV.16
VI. 44
VI.4 9
VI. 55
VII. 9
VII.24

-पथा : **–pathā**
VI. 60

पथिक : **pathika**
II. 72

पथिन् : **pathin**
IV. 78

पर : **para**
II. 31
III. 13
III. 34
III. 84
IV. 73
V. 24
V. 54
VIII. 24

परचित्तधीः : **paracittadhīḥ**
VII. 16

परत : **parata**
VIII. 23

परभाव : **parabhāva**
I. 18

परभेदन : **parabhedana**
IV. 76

परम : **parama**
IV. 9

-परमनोज्ञान : **–paramanojña**
VII. 11

परम् : **param**
III. 21
III. 76
III. 83
IV. 47

परलोक : **paraloka**
III. 19

परविज्ञपनादि : **paravijñapanādi**
IV. 26

परस्त्रीगमनाभिध्याऽदत्ता-दानसमापनः : **parastrīgaman-ābhidhyādattād-ānasamāpana**
IV. 70

परस्वविषमस्पृहा : **parasvaviṣamas-pṛhā**

IV. 77

परमा : paramā
(परम + आ)
(f)
VIII. 42

रमाणु : paramāṇu
II. 22
III. 85[2]

रमार्थशुभ : paramārthaśub ha
IV. 8

रमार्थसत् : paramārthasat
VI. 4

रा : parā
(f)
III. 32

-परार्थ- : –parārtha–
IV. 114

रावृत्तजन्मार्य : parāvṛttajanmā -rya
VI. 41

रामर्श : parāmarśa
V.16

-परामर्श : :–parāmarśa
V. 3

-पराश्रय : –parāśraya

III. 72

परिचित्तवित् : paricittavit
VII. 5

परिज्ञा : parijñā
(f)
V. 64
V. 65
V. 68

परिज्ञातादिनिश्चय : parijñātādiniśc- aya
VII. 7

-परिज्ञान : –parijñāna
V. 60

परिज्ञेय : parijñeya
VII. 7

परित्ताभ : parittābha
III. 77

परिरधावतः : paridhāvatah
III. 23

-परिनिर्वृति : –parinirvṛti
VI. 37

परिपूरक : paripūraka
IV. 95

परिपूरिन् : paripūrin
III. 20

-परिपूर्णत्व : –paripūrṇatva
VI. 65

परिपृच्छय : paripṛcchya
V. 22

परिभेदवत् : paribhedavat
III. 6

परिवार : parivāra
IV. 120

परिषण्ड : Pariṣaṇda
III. 63

परिष्कारलोभोत्थ : pariṣkāralobhot -tha
IV. 86

परिहाणि : parihāṇi
(f)
VI. 22
VI. 59

-परिहाणिभाक् : –parihāṇibhāk
VI. 41

-परीक्षण : –parikṣaṇa
VI. 14

परीत्तक्लेशभूमिका : paritiakleśabh- ūmikā
(f)
II. 27

परीत्ताभ : parīttābha
III. 81

परेण : pareṇa
V. 52

-पर्यन्त : –paryanta
III. 85

पर्यवस्थान : paryavasthāna
V. 47

-पर्यवस्थान : –paryavasthāna
V. 10

पर्यादान : paryādāna
II. 33

-पर्यास- : –paryāsa–
V. 9

-पर्व : –parva
III. 86

पर्वत : parvata
III. 64

पश्चात् : paścāt
III. 46
III. 102

पश्चिम : paścima
I. 38

पश्यति : paśyati
दृश्
I. 42
I. 43

पाक : pāka
IV. 48

पाञ्चविध्य : pāñcavidhya
VI. 43

प्रज्ञा : prajñā
(f)
I. 2
I. 33
VI. 12
VI. 15
VI. 64
VI. 68^2
VIII. 8

प्रज्ञाकार : prajñākāra
VII. 13

-प्रज्ञात्मक : –prajñātmaka
VII. 32

प्रज्ञोपक्लेशदेशन : prajñopakleśad-eśana
III. 29

-प्रणीधि- : –praṇidhi–
VII. 35

प्रणिधिज्ञान : praṇidhijñāna
(f)
VII. 37

प्रणीता : praṇītā
IV. 127

प्रतापन : pratāpana
III. 83

प्रति : prati
IV. 46

प्रतिक्षिप्त : pratikṣipta
IV. 122

प्रतिक्षेपणसावध : pratikṣepaṇasāv-adha
IV. 34

प्रतिध : pratigha
V.1

-प्रतिघ- : –pratigha–
V. 20
V. 23

प्रतिधज : pratighaja
V. 50

प्रतिघसंस्पर्श : pratighasaṁspa-rśa
III. 30

प्रतिघान्वय : pratighānvaya
V. 49

प्रतिपक्ष : pratipakṣa
I. 26
V. 61

-प्रतिपक्ष : pratipakṣa
VII. 8
VII. 9

प्रतिपक्षविर्निधावभावन : pratipakṣavinir-dhāvabhāvana
VII. 27

प्रतिपक्षोदय : pratipakṣodaya
V. 42
V. 60

प्रतिपक्षोदयफलप्राप्ती न्द्रियविवृद्धि : pratipakṣodaya-phalaprāptīndri-yavivṛdhi
V. 63

प्रतिपत्तार : pratipattāra
VIII. 39

प्रतिपत् : pratipat
VII. 29

प्रतिपत्सुख : pratipatsukha
VI. 66

प्रतिपन्नक : pratipannaka
VI. 31
VI. 32
VI. 44

-प्रतिपन्नक : –pratipannaka
VI.29
VI. 30
VI. 35

-प्रतिपन्न : –pratipanna
VI. 36

प्रतिपाद्य (प्रति +√पद्) : pratipādya
I. 27

प्रतिबिम्ब : pratibimba
III. 11

प्रतिभान : pratibhāna
VII. 37

प्रतिलम्भनिषेवाख्य : pratilaṁbhaniṣ-evākhya
VII. 27

प्रतिविज्ञप्ति : prativijñapti
(f)
I. 16

-प्रतिवृद्धि- : –prativṛddhi–
III. 84

प्रतिसंख्यानिरोध : pratisaṁkhyāni-rodha
I. 6

प्रतिसंधि : pratisaṅdhi
(f)
III. 24

-प्रतिसंविद्- : –pratisaṁvid–
VII. 35

प्रतीत्य : pratitya
प्रति +√इ
III. 20

प्रत्यय : pratyaya
II. 46

प्रविद : **pravida**
VIII. 12

प्रवृत्ति : **pravṛiti**
(f)
II. 6

प्रश्रब्धि : **praśrabdhi**
(f)
II. 25

प्रश्रब्धिशीलसंकल्प : **praśrabdhiśīlas-aṅkalpa**
(f)
VI. 68

-प्रसङ्ग : **–prasaṅga**
IV. 34

प्रसाद : **prasāda**
I. 9

-प्रसाद : **–prasāda**
IV. 54
VI. 73
VII. 54
VIII. 7
VIII. 9
VIII. 10

प्रसादक्लेशवेगवान् : **prasādakleśave-gavān**
IV. 22

प्रसिद्ध्यर्थ : **prasiddhyartha**
I. 17

प्रस्रब्धि : **prasrabhi**
(f)
VIII. 10

प्रस्रब्धिसुखमाद्य : **prasrabdhisukh-amādya**
VIII. 9

प्रहाण : **prahāṇa**
V. 69

-प्रहाण- : **–prahāṇa–**
VI. 60

-प्रहाण : **–prahāṇa**
VIII. 31

प्रहाणधातु : **prahāṇadhātu**
VI. 78

प्रहाणमार्ग : **prahāṇamārga**
IV. 87

प्रहाणाख्य : **prahāṇākhya**
IV. 18

प्रहाणाधारभूतत्व : **prahāṇādhārab-hūtatva**
V. 61

प्रहातव्य : **prahātavya**
V. 61

प्रहार : **prahāra**
IV. 104

प्रहीण : **prahiṇa**
V. 28²

प्रहीयन्ते : **parhīyante**
प्र + √हा
V. 4

-प्रहेय : **–praheya**
V. 29

प्राक् : **Prāc**
I. 23
II. 44
III. 22²
III. 23
III. 54
III. 90
III. 97
IV. 72
V. 28
VI. 42

प्राक्त : **prākta**
VI. 24

प्राङ्निविसच्युत : **prāṅginavisacy-uta**
VII. 30

-प्राण : **–prāṇa**
VIII. 43

प्राणातिपात : **prāṇātipāta**
IV. 73

प्रातिमोक्षक्रियापथ : **prātimokṣakriy-apath**
IV. 16

प्रातिमोक्षद : **prātimokṣada**
IV. 38

प्रातिमोक्षस्थित : **prātimokṣasthita**
IV. 19

प्रातिमोक्षाख्य : **prātimokṣākhya**
IV. 13
IV. 14
IV. 26

प्रातिमोक्षान्वित : **prātimokṣānvita**
IV. 17

प्रातिहार्य : **prātihārya**
VII. 47

प्राधान्य : **prādhānya**
I. 24
III. 25
IV. 124

प्रान्तकोटिक : **prāntakoṭika**
VII. 40

-प्राप्त- : **–prāpta–**
VI. 57

प्राप्ताप्राप्तोपभोगतः : **prāptāpraptopa-bhogataḥ**
VI. 59

प्राप्ति : **prāpti**
(f)
I. 2

फलहेत्वभिसंक्षेप : phatahetvabhisa-ṅkṣepa
III. 26

फलाद्यप्रतिपन्नक : phalādyapratipa-naka
VI. 29

फलप्त्युत्तप्तिहानि : phalāptyuttaptih-āni
IV. 40

बद्धत्व : baddhatva
VI. 75

बन्धनत्रय : bandhanatraya
V. 45

बल : bala
II. 58
VII. 30
VII. 32
VII. 43

-बल- : –bala–
VII. 30

-बल : –bala
VII.31²
VIII. 38

बलकाल : balakāla
VIII. 43

बल चौर्यतः : balacauryata
IV. 73

बलादय : baladaya
VII. 28

बहिः : bahiḥ
III. 49
III. 67

बहु : bahu
I. 24
II. 21

बहुविध : bahuvidha
III. 89

बाल : bāla
II. 20
IV. 52

बालिश : bāliśa
IV. 100

बाह्य : bāhya
I. 36
I. 48
III. 52

-बाह्य- : –bāhya–
III. 85
VI. 12
VII. 49

बाह्यक : bāhyaka
V. 21

-बीज- : –bija–
IV. 121

बीजवत् : bījavat
III. 36

बुद्ध : buddha
I. 1
IV. 104
IV. 122
VI. 1
VI. 23
VI. 62
VII. 1
VII. 41
VIII. 1

-बुद्ध : –buddha
VI. 74
VII. 34

बुद्धचेतन : buddhacetana
IV. 109

बुद्धतत्संध : buddhatatsaṅgha
VI. 74

बुद्धत्व : buddhattva
III. 94

बुद्धधर्म : buddhadharma
VII. 28

बुद्धोऽप्रयोगतः : buddhoprayoga-taḥ

VII. 6

बुद्धवत् : buddhavat
III. 96

बुद्धसंधकर : buddhasaṃgha-kara
IV. 32

बुद्धि : buddhi
VI. 4

बृहत्फल : bṛhatfala
II. 41

बोधि : bodhi
(f)
VI. 67
VI. 76

बोधिमार्गाङग्वर्जित : bodhimārgāṅga-varjita
VI. 73

बोधिलभ्या : bodhilabhyā
(f)
II. 44

बोध्यङ्गमार्गअङ्ग : bodhyaṇgamārgāṇgu
VI. 71

बोधिसत्व : bodhisattva
IV. 106
IV. 108
IV. 117
IV. 118

-भावतः : –bhāvataḥ
IV. 84
V. 16

भावन : bhāvana
VI.70

-भावन : –bhāvana
VI.1
VII. 27^2

भावना : bhāvanā
I. 40
II. 13
IV. 123
IV. 124
IV. 124
V. 6
V. 10
VI. 5
VII. 25

-भावना : –bhāvanā
V. 10
VI. 29
VI. 34

-भावना : –bhāvanā
II. 9
V. 6
VI. 14
VI. 53
VII. 22^2
VII. 24
VII.25
VIII.27
VIII.28

भावनाज : bhāvanāja
VII. 53

भावनापथ : bhāvanāpatha
VII. 9

भावनामय : bhāvanāmaya
VI. 20

भावनामार्ग : bhāvanāmārga
VI. 1

भावनास्थ : bhāvanāstha
V. 69

भावनाहेय : bhāvanāheya
IV. 11
V. 5
V. 52

भावनाहेयकर्मन् : bhāvanāheyaka-rman
IV. 93

भावलक्षणावस्थाऽन्यथाऽन्यथिकसंज्ञित : bhāvalakṣaṇāva-sthānyathānyat-hikasaṃjñita
V. 26

-भाव- : –bhāva–
I. 18
IV. 83
V. 37

-भावित : –bhāvita
VII. 23

भाव्यते √भू : bhāvyate
VII. 26^2

भाव्यन्ते √भू : bhāvyante
VII. 20

भाषण : bhāṣaṇa
VII. 51

भिक्षु : bhikṣu
IV. 100

-भिक्षुता- : –bhikṣutā–
IV. 15

भिक्षुवत् : bhikṣuvat
IV. 30

भित्वा √भिद् : bhitvā
II. 71

भिनत्ति √भिद् : bhinatti
IV. 100

भिन्न : bhinna
IV. 76
IV. 82
IV. 100
VI. 3

-भुजा : –bhujā
VI. 48

-भुव : –bhuva
II. 52
V. 13

-भू- : –bhū–
VII. 44
VIII. 34

-भू : –bhū
VI. 11
VI. 12
VII. 39

भूत : bhūta
I. 12
II. 44
II. 65^2
IV. 5

-भूत- : –bhūta–
IV. 125

-भूतजा : –bhūtajā
IV. 4
IV. 6^2

-भूतत्व : –bhūtava
V. 61

भूतवत्चित्तचित्तानुवर्त्ति-लक्षणलक्ष्यम् : bhūtavatcittacit-tānuvartilakṣa-ṇ-alakṣyam
II. 50

भूतशीलप्रदेशाध्वद्वयान : bhūtaśīlapradeś -ādhvadvayāna
V. 62

भूमि : bhūmi
IV. 46
IV. 55
V. 56
VI. 33^2
VIII. 14
VIII. 18

भूमि- : –bhūmi–
VI. 91
V. 15
VIII. 2
VIII. 17
VII. 23

भूमि : –bhūmi
I.47
II. 52^2
II. 54
III. 7
III. 71
IV.26
VI. 66
VII. 21
VII. 30
VII. 41
VIII. 19

भूमिक : –bhūmika
I. 47
III. 2^2
III. 38
V. 15
V. 36
V. 56
VI. 20
VI. 27
VII. 51
VII. 54
VIII. 15

-भूमिका : –bhūmikā
II. 27
IV. 91
V. 54

भूमित्याग : bhūmityāga
VI. 21

भूमिसंचारहानि : bhūmisaṁchār-ahāni
IV. 40

भूम्यक्षपुद्गलोत्क्रान्त : bhūmyakṣapud -galotkrānta
VII. 5

भूमी : bhūmi
(f)
VI. 61

भूय : bhuya
III. 50

भूयः : bhūyaḥ
VI. 6

भूयसा : bhūyasā
VIII. 41

-भूषित : –bhūṣita
III. 67

भूसंचार : bhusaṁcāra
II. 40

भृत : bhṛta
III. 98

भेतृ : bhetṛ
IV. 99

-भेद : –bheda
III. 1
IV. 59
IV. 98
IV. 101^2
IV. 102
IV. 105
V. 2
V. 41
VII. 4
VIII. 28

-भेदतस् : –bhedatas
II. 23

-भेदतः : –bhedataḥ
VI. 33

-भेदन : –bhedana
IV. 76
IV. 107

भोग : bhoga
III. 23^2

-भोग : –bhoga
IV. 71

-भोग्य- : –bhogya–
IV. 113

भौतिक : bhautika
I. 35
II. 65^2

भौतिकार्थ्य : bhautikārthya
I. 23

भ्रमति : bhramati

भ्रम्
I. 3

भ्रूमध्य : bhrūmadhya
VI. 11

-भ्रष्ट : –bhraṣṭa
IV. 94
VI. 60

मग्न : magna
III. 50

मण्डल : maṅḍala
III.55

-मण्डल : –maṅḍala
III. 47

मत : mata
I. 16
I. 44
II. 3
II. 30
II. 38

III. 28
III. 73
IV. 65
IV. 75
IV. 96
IV. 101
IV. 105
V. 5
V. 61
VI. 40
VI. 43
VI. 56
VIII. 42

-मत : –mata
VII. 7

मता : matā
IV. 57
IV. 85

मति : mati
(f)
II. 24
V. 20

-मति- : –mati–
VII. 7

-मति : –mati
III. 15
VI. 50
VI. 66

मत्सर : matsara
II. 27

-मत्सर : –matsara
V. 48

मद : mada
II. 27
II. 33
IV. 29
V. 49
V. 58

-मद : –mada
V. 50
V. 53

मद्य : madya
IV. 34

मध्य : madhya
III. 26
III. 66
IV. 21

-मध्य- : –madhya–
III.66
VI. 33

-मध्य : –madhya
VI. 33
IV.25
IV.11

मध्या : madhyā
(f)
II. 8
VI. 59

मध्ये : madhye
III. 20

मध्यम : madhyama
III. 55
III. 74
IV. 48

IV. 90[2]

मध्यमा : madhyamā
IV. 41

मध्ययान्वित : madhyayānvita
IV. 23

मध्यस्थ : madhyastha
IV. 21
IV. 25

मध्याह्न : madhyāhna
III. 60

मनइन्द्रियसंवर : manaindriyasaṁvara
IV. 18

मनस् : manas
I. 5
I. 16[2]
I. 17
I. 31[2]
I. 43
I. 47
II. 11[2]
II. 13
II. 15
II. 20
II. 34
II. 66
IV.31
IV. 64
VI. 13

-मनस्- : –manas–
II. 17
II. 20

IV. 65
IV. 75
V. 55
VII. 11
VII. 45
VII.42

मनस्कार : manaskar
II. 24
V. 34

-मनस्कार : –manaska
VI. 11

मनश्चित्ते : manaśacitte
IV. 58

मनश्च्युति : manścyuti
(f)
III. 43

मनापा : manāpā
(f)
VI. 3

मनुष्य : manuṣya
III. 1

मनुष्यज : manuṣyaja
VIII. 37

मनोजवा : manojavā
(f)
VII. 48

मनोपविचारतः : manopavicārtas

III. 32

मनोमय : manomaya
III. 40

मातृपितृग्लानधार्मकथिक : **mātṛpitṛglānad-hārmakathika**
IV. 118

मात्सर्य : **mātsarya**
V. 42
V. 57

-मात्सर्य- : **–mātsarya–**
V. 47

मान : **māna**
II. 33
V. 1
V. 10
V. 16
V. 33

-मान- : **–mān–**
V. 21
V. 45

-मान : **–mān**
V. 23

मानस : **mānasa**
IV. 1
IV. 11
V. 24

मानसी : **mānasī**
I. 33^2

मान्द्य : **māndya**
VIII. 4

माया : **māyā**
(f)
II. 27
V. 49
V. 53
V. 58

मायामद : **māyāmada**
V. 50

मारण : **māraṇa**
IV. 73

-मारण : **–māraṇ**
IV. 85
IV. 106

मालाधारा : **mālādhārā**
III. 64

मास : **māsa**
III. 61

-मास : **–māsa**
III. 89
III. 99

-मासक : **–māsaka**
III. 89

मासाह्न : **māsāhana**
III. 83

मिथःफल : **mithaḥphala**
II. 50

-मिथ्या- : **–mithyā–**
IV. 74
V. 3

मिथ्याचार : **mithyācāra**
IV. 33

मिथ्याजीव : **mithyājīva**
IV. 86

मिथ्यात्वनियत : **mithyātvaniyata**
III. 44

मिथ्यादृग्विमती : **mithyādṛgvimatī**
(f)
V. 14

मिथ्यादृष्टि : **mithyādṛṣṭi**
(f)
IV. 71
IV. 78
IV. 82
V. 32

मिद्ध : **middha**
II. 30
II. 31
V. 58

म्रियते : **mriyate**
मृ
VI. 60

-मिश्र- (मिश्रकावन?) : **–miśra–**
III. 67

-मिश्रण : **–miśraṇa**
VI. 42

मिश्रत्व : **miśratva**
VI. 53

मिश्रिता : **miśritā**
(f)
V. 38

मुक्त : **mukta**
IV. 117^2

-मुक्त- : **–mukta–**
मुच्
III. 39
VII. 38

-मुक्त : **–mukta**
VI.34
VI. 57

मुक्ति : **mukti**
(f)
VI. 48

-मुक्ति : **–mukti**
VII. 24
VII. 25

-मुक्ती- : **–muktī–**
(f)
VI.65

मुक्तिमार्ग : **muktimārga**
VI. 28
VI. 51

मुक्तिमार्गधीः : **muktimārgadhīḥ**
(f)
VII. 42

मैत्री : **maitrī**
(f)
VIII. 29

-मैत्री- : **–maitrī–**
IV. 56

मैथुन : **maithuna**
III. 23[2]

-मैथुन : **–maithuna**
III. 69

मैथुनरागिन् : **maithunarāgin**
III. 23

मोक्ष : **mokṣa**
IV. 8
IV. 127
V. 44
VI. 24

-मोक्ष- : **–mok-**
V. 2

मोक्षभागीय : **mokṣabhāgiya**
VI. 24

मोदन : **modana**
IV. 124

मोदन्ताम् : **modantām**
√मुद्
VIII. 30

मोह : **moha**
I. 20
II. 26
IV. 71
V. 19
V. 35
V. 55

-मोह : **–moha**
V. 21
V. 45

-मोहज : **–mohaja**
IV. 69

मोहाकाङ्क्षा : **mohākāṅkṣā**
V. 32

मौनत्रय : **mounatraya**
IV. 64

मौल : **maula**
III. 35
IV. 35
IV. 72
VIII. 5
VIII. 21

मौला : **maulā**
(f)
V. 66

मौलि : **mauli**
VI. 22

म्रक्ष : **mrakṣa**
II. 27
V. 48
V. 58

-म्रक्ष : **–mrakṣa**
V.48

यः : **yaḥ**
(यद् पुं)
I. 1
I. 6
I. 10
I. 39
II. 45
III. 10
IV. 32
V. 18
VI. 31
VI. 79
VIII. 28

यतः : **yataḥ**
I. 3
I. 42
IV. 46
IV. 48
IV. 108
V. 42
VI. 13
VI. 61
VI. 63
VII. 30

यत्र : **yatra**
IV. 5
V. 23
VI. 4
VI. 31

यथा : **yathā**
I. 22
I. 27[2]
IV. 31
IV. 33
IV. 112
V. 38
V. 56
VI. 2
VI. 3
VI. 15
VII. 20
VII. 32

यथाक्रम : **yathākrama**
II. 60
III. 17
III. 41
III. 82
III. 99
III. 100
IV. 29
IV. 60
IV. 64
IV. 75
IV. 94
IV. 126
V. 4
VI. 28

VI. 49
VI. 70
VII. 38
VII. 50
VIII. 17

यथाक्षेप : **yathākṣepa**
III. 19

यथाभूतसूत्राद्याक्लष्ट-देशना : **yathābhūtasūtr -ādyākliṣṭadeśa nā**
IV. 125

यथायोग : **yathāyoga**
IV. 66

यथार्थ : **yathārtha**
I. 1

यथास्थान : **yathāsthāna**
I. 23

यथोक्त : **yothokta**
II. 10

यथोदिता : **yathodita**
(f)
VI. 76

यत् (यद् पुं) : **yat**
I. 2

यद् (यद्-पुं) : **yad**
I. 17

II. 58^{2}
IV. 52

यत् : **yat**
IV. 54^{2}
IV. 55
IV. 75
IV. 87
IV. 88
IV. 103
VII. 9

यद् : **yad**
VII. 26^{2}

यत् : **yat**
VII. 56
VIII. 13

यद्दुर्गृहीत : **yaddurgṛhita**
VIII. 40

यद्वत् : **yadvat**
VII. 43

यदि : **yadi**
VI. 50

यव : **yava**
III. 86

यशस्विन् : **yaśasvin**
IV. 116

यस्मात् (यद् पुं) : **yasmāt**
I. 4
IV. 2

V. 39
V. 42

या (यद् स्त्री) : **yā**
I. 2
II. 7
II. 72
IV. 61
IV. 62
V. 12^{2}
VII. 1

याति √या : **yāti**
III. 15
III. 19
IV. 32

यात्निक : **yātnika**
VII. 21

यानि (यद् नपुं) : **yāni**
I. 25

यावत् : **yāvat**
II. 5
III. 70
III. 72
III. 76
III. 90
III. 91

IV. 12
IV. 22
IV. 81^{2}
IV. 108
V. 69
VI. 30
VII. 50
VIII. 15

यावज्जीव : **yāvajjīva**
IV. 27

युक्त युज् : **yukta**
II. 20
II. 21
II. 21
VI. 21

-युक्त- : **–yukta–**
IV.38

-युक्त : **–yukta**
II. 17
II. 29
IV. 9

युक्ता : **yuktā**
(f)
V. 14

युग : **yuga**
IV. 102

युगन्धर : **yugaṅdhara**
III. 48

युगपत् : **yugapat**
IV. 81

ये : **ye**
(यद् पुं)
I. 8
I. 48
II. 50
IV. 56
V. 13
V. 46
VIII. 34

येन : **yena**
IV. 113
V. 18

येषाम् : **yeṣām**
(यद् पुं)
III. 87

योग : **yoga**
I. 27
VI. 3

-योग : **–yoga**
IV. 66
V. 27
V. 37
VI.3

योगप्रवर्तित : **yogapravartita**
IV. 126

योजन : **yojana**
III. 88

-योजन : **–yojana**
III. 54
III. 60
III. 66

योजना : **yojanā**
VII. 47

योजनार्ध : **yojanārdha**
III. 76

योज्य : **yojya**
VII. 17

योनि : **yoni**
(f)
III. 8

रक्त : **rakta**
II. 33

रण्य : **raṇya**
III. 87

रत : **rata**
VIII. 24

रत्नशिखिन् : **ratnaśikhin**
IV. 110

रवि : **ravi**
III. 62

रस : **rasa**
I. 10
I. 30

रसराग : **rasarāga**
III. 97

राग : **rāga**
V. 2

-राग- : **–rāga–**
V. 1

-राग : **–rāga**
V. 16
V. 33
V. 45
V. 55
V. 2
V.22

रागज : **rāgaja**
IV. 59

-रागज : **–rāgaja**
V. 50

रागप्रतिघमान : **rāgapratigham-āna**
V. 23

रागप्रतिघमूढय : **rāgapratigham-ooḍhaya**
V. 20

रागसंक्षय : **rāgasaṁkṣaya**
VI. 78

रागिन् : **rāgin**
II. 21
IV. 111

-रागिन् : **–rāgin**
III. 23
VI. 9
VII. 19

रागोत्थ : **rāgottha**
V. 48

-रात्र- : **–rātra–**
III. 89

-रात्र : **–rātra**
III. 60
III. 79
III. 82
IV. 27^2

रात्रयहर्वृद्धी : **rātryaharvṛddhi**
III. 62

राशि : **raśi**
(f)
I. 20

रिरंसा : **riraṁsā**
(f)
III. 15

रूचि : **rūci**
(f)
I. 20

रूचित्र : **rūcitra**
IV. 115

रूज : **ruja**
IV. 99

लक्ष्येते : lakṣyete
लक्ष्
VI. 13

लक्षत्रय : lakṣatraya
III. 53

लक्षद्वादशक : lakṣadvādaśaka
III. 47

लक्षषोडशक : lakṣaṣodaśaka
III. 45

-लक्षोच्छ्र्य : –lakṣochrya
III. 46

लङ्घिता : laṅghitā
(f)
VIII. 18

-लज्जित्व : –lajjittva
IV. 97

लपनागीतनाट्यवत् : lapanāgītanāṭy-avat
IV. 77

लब्धा : labdha
VI. 6

लब्धपूर्व : labdhapūrva
VII. 26

लभते : labhate
√लभ्
VI. 21
VIII. 14

लभ्यते : labhyate
√लभ्
II. 14
IV. 26

लभ्या : labhyā
(f)

-लभ्या : –labhyā
II. 44
VII. 44

-लव : –lava
III. 88

लवशः : lavaśaḥ
III. 62

लाभ : lābha
I. 38
II. 36
II. 73
IV. 33
IV. 37[2]
VI. 32
VI. 53
VI. 74
VII. 26
VII. 50

-लाभ : –lābha
V.63
VI. 64

लाभतः : lābhataḥ
√लभ्
IV. 83
IV. 84

-लाभतः : –lābhataḥ
V. 70

-लाभिक : –lābhika
VII. 56

-लभितृ : –labhitṛ
IV. 115

-लाभिन् : –labhin
IV. 79
VI. 23[2]
VI. 43

-लाभी : –lābhī
VII. 40

-लिक्ष् : –likṣa
III. 86

लिङगृतस् : liṅgatas
IV. 14

लिपिमुद्रा : lipimudrā
IV. 126

लोक : loka
I. 3
I. 8
III. 92
IV. 105

-लोक- : –loka–
III. 73

-लोक : –loka
III.1 9
III. 45

लोकचक्षुष् : lokacakṣuṣ
VIII. 41

लोकधातु : lokadhātu
III. 74

लोकवैचित्र्य : lokavaicitrya
IV. 1

लोकसंज्ञा : lokasaṁjñā
(f)
I. 13

लोकोत्तर : lokottara
VI. 45
VI. 46
VIII. 6

-लोभ- : –lobha–
IV. 86

लोभज : lobhaja
IV. 86

लोभतः : lobhatā
IV. 70

लोहापृशशाविगोच्छिद्रर-जोलिक्षास्तदुद्भव : lohāpśaśāvigoc-chidraraiolikṣās-tadudbhava
III. 86

लौकिक : laukika
V. 67

विदित्वा : **viditvā**
VIII. 43

विदुः : **viduḥ**
विद्
IV. 63

विदेहः : **videhaḥ**
III. 54
III. 56

विद्या : **vidyā**
(f)
III. 28
III. 31
VII. 45
VII. 46

-विद्या- : **–vidyā–**
VII. 56

विद्यादनात्मतः : **vidyādanātmat aḥ**
VII. 18

विद्वश : **vidvaśa**
V. 45

-विद्वेष : **–vidveṣa**
IV. 78

-विध : **–vidha**
IV. 53

विधा : **vidhā**
(f)
VI. 55

विधादि : **vidhādi**
V. 11

विधिभ्रष्ट : **vidhibhraṣṭa**
IV. 94

विना : **vinā**
I. 30
II. 46
V. 35
VI. 19

विनाशक : **vināśaka**
IV. 3

विनितक : **vinitaka**
III. 49

-विनिर्धाव : **–vinirdhāva**
VII. 27

-विनिवृत्ति : **–vinivṛtti**
(f)
III. 25

विपक्ष : **vipakṣa**
III. 28
IV. 123
VI. 7

-विपक्ष- : **–vipakṣa–**
V. 59

-विपक्षतः : **–vipakṣataḥ**
IV. 120
VI. 8
VI. 15
VIII. 29

विपरीततः : **viparītataḥ**
V. 9

विपर्यय : **viparyaya**
II. 63
III. 5
III. 61
IV. 9
IV. 66
IV. 68
V. 55
V. 57
VII. 52

विपर्यस्तमति : **viparyastamati**
(f)
III. 15

-विपर्यास : **–viparyāsa**
VI.7

विपर्यास : **viparyāsa**
V. 8

विपर्यासविपक्षतः : **viparyasavipak-ṣataḥ**
VI. 15

विपश्यति : **vipaśyati**
वि+√दृष्
VI. 16

विपश्यिन् : **vipaśyin**
IV. 110

विपाक : **vipāka**
II. 10
II. 14
II. 41
II. 48
II. 57
II. 60
IV. 55
IV. 57
IV. 20

-विपाक- : **–vipāka–**
IV. 85

विपाकज : **vipākaja**
I. 37
II. 60
II. 72
IV. 12

-विपाकज : **–vipākaja**
IV. 58

विपाकजा : **vipākajā**
I. 37

विपाकतः : **vipākataḥ**
IV. 48

विपाकतः : **vipākataḥ**
IV. 49

विपाकफल : **vipākaphala**
II. 56

पाकहेतु : **vipākahetu**
II. 54

पाकाख्य : **vipākākhya**
II. 49

विपादन : **–vipādana**
IV. 103

प्रयुक्त : **viprayukta**
II. 35

प्रयुक्तक : **viprayuktaka**
IV. 98

भज्य : **vibhajya**
V. 21

भवेच्छा : **vibhavechhā**
V. 11

भाषा : **vibhāṣā**
IV. 36

भूतरूपसंज्ञाख्य : **vibhutarupasaṁjñākhya**
VIII. 3

वेभ्रम : **vibhrama**
V. 44

मति : **vimati**
V. 12

वेमति : **–vimati**
V. 14

मान : **vimāna**
III. 69

विमानोदयव्यय : **vimanodayavyaya**
III. 101

-विमुक्त- : **–vimukta–**
VI. 47

-विमुक्त : **–vimukta**
VI. 64

विमुक्ति : **vimukti**
(f)
VI. 49
VI. 56
VI. 60
VI. 75

-विमुक्ति : **–vimukti**
VI. 63

विमुक्ती : **vimuktī**
VI. 76

विमुच्यते
वि +√मुच् : **vimuchyate**
VI. 77

विमोक्ष : **vimokṣa**
VIII. 32

विमोक्षमुखत्रय : **vimokṣamukhatraya**
VIII. 25

-विमोक्षवत् : **–vimokṣavat**
VIII. 35

वियोग : **viyoga**
I. 18

-वियोग : **–viyoga**
V. 68

विरक्त : **virakta**
IV. 52
VI. 30

विरज्यते
वि+√रञ्ज् : **virajyate**
VI. 79

विरति : **virati**
IV. 122

विरतिग्रह : **viratigraha**
IV. 15

विराग : **virāga**
VI. 78

विरागतः : **virāgataḥ**
VII. 44

विवसति
वि+√वस् : **vivasati**
IV. 100

-विवर्जित : **–vivarjita**
II. 72
V. 4
V. 13
VII. 12

विवर्तकल्प : **vivartakalpa**
III. 90

विवर्तते
वि+√वृत् : **vivartate**
III. 93

विवाद : **vivāda**
I. 36
V. 48

विवादमूल : **vivādamūla**
I. 21

विवृत : **vivṛta**
III. 92

-विवृद्धि : **vivṛddhi**
V. 63

-विवेकज : **–vivekaja**
VIII. 2

-विवेचन : **vivecana**
V. 38

विशति
√विश् : **viśati**
III. 16

विशदत्व : **viśadatva**
III. 17

विशिष्ट : **viśiṣṭa**
II. 52[2]

-विशिष्ट : **–viśiṣṭa**

व्यवस्थित : vyavasthita
V. 26

व्याकरण : vyākaraṇa
V. 22

व्याकृत : vyākṛta
III. 43

-व्याकृत : –vyākṛta
IV. 98

व्याकृतोद्भव : vyākṛtodbhava
II. 57

व्यापाद : Vyāpāda
III. 31
IV. 78

-व्यापाद- : –Vyāpāda–
IV. 70

-व्यापाद : –Vyāpāda
IV. 82

व्यापादादिविपक्षत: : vyāpādādivipak-ṣataḥ
VIII. 29

-व्यावृत्ति : –vyāvṛtti
(f)
V. 2

व्युत्क्रान्तकसमापत्तिर्विसभागतृतीयगा : vyutkrāntakasamāpattirvisabh-āgatṛtiyagā
(f)
VIII. 19

व्युत्थान : vyutthāna
VIII. 33

-व्रत- : –vrata–
V. 3

व्रताड्.ग : vratāṅga
IV. 29

व्रीहिसन्तानसाधर्म्यादविच्छिन्नभवोदभव : vrīhisantānasād-harmyādavicchi-nnabhavodbhava
III. 11

शंकला : śaṅkalā
(f)
VI. 9

शकटाकृति : śakaṭākṛti
(f)
III. 53

शक्तित: : śaktitaḥ
III. 22

शण्ढादी : śaṇḍhādi
IV. 97

शण्डपण्डद्विधाकृति : śaṇḍapaṇḍadvid-hākṛti
IV. 43

-शत- : –śata–
III. 54
III. 94

-शत : –śata
III. 88
IV. 109

शतचतुष्टय : śatacatuṣṭaya
III. 47

-शतज : –śataja
IV. 110

शतपञ्चक : śatapañcaka
III. 83

शताद्यावत् : śatādyāvat
III. 94

शनै: : śanaiḥ
III. 97

शब्द : śabda
I. 10
I. 34
I. 37

शब्दक : śabadaka
I. 29

-शमथ : –śamatha
VI. 14

शरण : śaraṇa
IV. 30
IV. 32

शरणत्रय : śaraṇatraya
IV. 32

-शश- : –śaśa–
III. 86

शस्त्ररोग : śastraroga
III. 99

शाक्यमुनि : śākyamuni
IV. 110

शाठ्य : Śāṭhyā
II. 27
V. 49
V. 51
V. 53
V. 58

शाठ्यद्वेषजरागज : śāṭhyadveṣajarāgaja
IV. 59

शातृ : śātṛ
II. 7

शान्तत: : śāntatotaṇ
VIII. 26

शान्तशुद्धयग्रभावत: : śāntaśudhyagra-bhāvataḥ
V. 16

शान्तादि : śāntādi
VI. 49

शान्ति : śānti

VI. 63
VII. 1
VII. 14^2
VII. 22
VII. 24
VII. 29
VII. 39
VII. 40
VIII. 31

षट्क्लेशमल : ṣaṭkleśamala
V. 49

षड्गोत्र : ṣaḍgotra
VI. 58

षड्भूमिनवभूमिकः : ṣadbhūminava-bhūmika
V. 15

षड्राग : ṣaḍrāga
V. 1

षड्रागभेद : ṣadrāgabheda
V. 2

षड्विध : ṣaḍvidha
II. 49
VII. 41

षड्विधा : ṣaḍvidhā
(f)
VI. 12
VII. 42

षड्विज्ञप्ति : ṣaḍvijñapti
IV. 67

षड्विज्ञानाश्रय : ṣaḍvijñānāśraya
V. 54

षड्वेदना : ṣadvedanā
(f)
III. 32

षट्सप्तज्ञानभावना : ṣaṭsaptajñānab h-āvanā
(f)
VII. 24

षष्टिर्लव : ṣaṣtirlava
III. 88

षष्ठ : ṣaṣtha
III. 30

-षष्ठ- : –ṣaṣṭha–
VI. 35

षष्ठी : ṣaṣṭhī
VII. 47

षोडश : ṣodaśa
III. 63
VI. 31
VII. 12
VII. 22

-षोडशक : –ṣodaśaka
III. 45

षोडशचित्त : ṣodaśacitta
VI. 27

षोडशाकार : ṣodaśākāra
VI. 17
VII. 10
VII. 13

षोडशाकारभावना : ṣodaśākārabhā-vanā
VI. 53

षोड्शोत्सद : ṣodśotsada
III. 58

षोढ : ṣodha
I. 10

संकलन : saṅkalana
V. 70

-संकलन : –saṅkalana
VI.52

संकल्प : saṅkalpa
VI. 52
VI. 72

-संकल्प : –saṅkalpa
VI. 68

संक्लेश (स) : saṁkleśa
I. 22
II. 1
II. 3
II. 5

-संक्षय : –saṁkṣaya

V. 60
V. 64
VI. 78

-संक्षेप- : –saṁkṣepa–
VI. 10

संख्या : saṁkhyā
I. 6

-संख्या- : –saṁkhyā–
IV. 126

संग्रह : saṁgraha
I. 24
III. 8

-संग्रह : –saṁgraha
I.1 8
I. 25

सङ्.ग्रह : saṁgraha
IV. 66

संघ : saṅgha
IV. 98

-संघ- : –saṅgha–
IV. 32

-संघ : –saṅgha
VI. 74

संघभेद : saṅghabheda
IV. 98
IV. 105

संघायद्वारहारिका : saṅghāyadvār-ahārikā
IV. 106

संप्राप्ति : saṁprāpti
(f)
II. 4

संभव : saṁbhava
II. 17
III.90

-संभव : –saṁbhava
III. 74
IV. 104
VI. 52

संभवति : saṁbhavati
सं +√भू
III. 70

संभवन्ति : saṁbhavanti
सं +√भू
V. 11

संभवैषिन् : saṁbhavaiṣin
III. 40

संभार : saṁbhāra
II. 5

संभाराकारगोचर : saṁbhārākāra-gocara
VII. 33

संभारधर्मकाया : saṁbhāradharmakāyā
VII. 34

संभूति : saṁbhūti
IV. 69

-संमित : –saṁmita
III. 80

संमुख : saṁmukha
IV. 109

संमुखीभाव : saṁmukhībhāva
IV. 83

संमुखीभावतस् : saṁmukhībhāv-atas
IV. 49

संमुखीभावतः : saṁmukhībhāv-ataḥ
IV. 84

संमोहविनिवृत्ति : saśmohavinivṛtti
(f)
III. 25

संयुक्त : saṁyukta
V. 28

संयुत : saṁyuta
V. 23
V. 24

संयोजनद्वय : saṁyojanadvaya
V. 42

संयोजनादिभेद : saṁyojanādibh-eda
V. 41

संयोजनादिवचन : saṁyojanādiva-cana
III. 29

संयोजनान्तर : saṁyojanāntara
V. 41

संवत्सर : saṁvatsara
III. 89

संवर : saṁvara
II. 51
IV. 13^2
IV. 16
IV. 22
IV. 33
IV. 35
IV. 36
IV. 43

-संवर : –saṁvara
IV. 18

-संवर्त- : –saṁvarta–
III. 74

संवर्त्तकल्प : saṁvartakalpa
III. 90

संवर्तते : saṁvartate
सम् +√वृत्
III. 93

संवर्तनी : saṁvartanī
(f)
III. 100

-संवर्तनी : –saṁvartanī
III. 102

-संवरवान् : –saṁvaravān
IV. 20

संवराप्तिमृत्युद्विव्यञ्ज-नोदय : saṁvarāptimṛty-udvivyañjanod-aya
IV. 41

संवित् : saṁvit
(f)
VII. 37

-संवित् : –saṁv
VII. 39

संवृत् : saṁvṛt
IV. 30

संवृत : saṁvṛta
IV. 31

संवृत्त : saṁvṛtta
III. 93

संवृति : saṁvṛti
IV. 27

संवृतिज्ञान : saṁvṛtijñāna
VII. 29
VII. 36
VII. 43

संवृतिज्ञापक : saṁvṛtijñāpaka
VII. 2

स्मृत : smṛta
I. 17
I. 48
II. 62
III. 89
V. 39
VI. 10
VI. 39

-स्मृत : –smṛta
VI. 9

स्मृता : smṛtā
(f)
III. 6

स्मृति : smṛti
(f)
I. 33
II. 24
VI. 14
VI. 68^2
VII. 16
VIII. 8
VIII. 10

-स्मृति- : –smṛti–
(f)
VIII. 8
VIII. 10

-स्मृती- : –smṛtī–
VI. 16

-स्मृति : –smṛti
IV. 18

स्मृति : smṛti
(f)
VI. 12

स्मृतिनाश : smṛtināśa
IV. 29

स्मृतिप्रज्ञात्मक : smṛtiprajñātm-aka
VII. 32

स्यात् (अस्) : syāt
I. 38
II. 30
IV. 3^3
IV. 12
IV. 103
V. 23
VI. 23

स्वः : svaḥ
III. 34

स्व : sva
III. 34^2
IV. 5
V. 56^2
VII. 10^2
VIII. 16

-स्व- : –sva–
IV. 73
IV. 77
VII. 11
VIII. 17
VIII. 34

स्वकलाप : svakalāpa
VII. 18

स्वकत्रय : svakatraya
V. 29

स्वकत्रयैकरूपाप्तामलविज्ञानगोचर : svakatrayaikrū-pāptāmalavijñā-nagocara
V. 29

स्वकर्मकृत् : svakarmakṛta
I. 39

स्वकाधरत्रयोर्ध्वैकामल : svakādharatray-ordhvaikāmala
V. 30

-स्वीक्रिया : –svīkriyā
IV. 73

स्वाक्षमुक्तननुग्रह : svāksmuktaran-ugraha
III. 39

स्वचतुःस्कन्धगोचर : svacatuḥskandh-agocara
VIII. 36

स्वच्छाया : svacchāyā
(f)
III. 62

स्वतः : svataḥ
II. 50
IV. 8
VII. 50

स्वतन्त्र : svatantra
V. 42
V. 52
V. 54

स्वदृष्टि : svadṛṣṭi
V. 33

स्वधातुक : svadhātuka
II. 37

स्वाधिकगोचर : svādhikagocara
V. 31

स्वाध्विक : svādhvika
V. 24

समम् : **samam**
III. 93

समं : **samam**
IV. 72

समः : **samaḥ**
III. 55

-समग्राङग् : **-samagrāṅga**
IV. 28

समता : **samatā**
(f)
VII. 34

समत्व : **samatva**
VII. 33

समनन्तर : **samanantara**
II.62

समनुप्रवेश : **samanupraveśa**
I. 2

समनुशेरते (सम् + अनु + शी) : **samanuśerate**
I. 4

समन्ततः : **samantatah**
III. 48

समन्वय : **samanvaya**
II. 36

-समन्वय : **–samanvaya**
VI. 47

समन्वागमत : **samanvāgamata**
IV. 82

समविशिष्ट : **samaviśiṣṭa**
II. 52^2

समन्वित : **samanvita**
IV. 24
IV. 98
IV. 99
V. 69

समल : **samala**
IV. 87
VII. 11

समसंवर्तसंभव : **samasaṁvartas-aṁbhava**
III. 74

समस्तालम्बन : **samastālambana**
VI. 16

समाकार : **samākāra**
VIII. 24

समादान : **samādāna**
IV. 27

-समाधय : **–samādhaya**
VIII. 25

समाधि : **samādhi**
(f)
II. 24
VI. 68
VI. 69
VII. 48

-समाधि : **–samādhi**
VIII. 7
VIII. 8
VIII. 23

समाधि : **samādhi**
IV. 112

समाधिज : **samādhija**
IV. 6
IV. 67

समाधिभावना : **samādhibhāvanā**
(f)
VIII. 27

समानसिद्धा : **samānasiddhā**
(f)
V. 54

समानुष : **samānuṣa**
III. 71

-समापन : **–samāpana**
IV. 70

समापत्ती : **samāpattī**
(f)
II. 42
II. 48
II. 64
VI. 64
VIII. 1
VIII. 33

समापत्ति : **samāpatti**
(f)
II. 35
IV. 95

-समापत्ति : **–samāpatti**
VI. 63
VIII. 19

समापत्तिद्रव्य : **samāpattidrv-aya**
VIII. 5

समाप्ति : **samāpti**
IV. 120

समारोप : **samāropa**
V. 9

समाश्रय : **samāśraya**
II. 53

सर्वत्र : **sarvatra**
II. 16
IV. 51
IV. 83
IV. 111
V. 24^3
VII. 39

सर्वत्रग : **sarvatraga**
II. 54
II. 55
II. 56

सर्वत्रगा : **sarvatragā**
V. 12
V. 17

सर्वत्रगो : **sarvatrago**
II. 49

सर्वथा : **sarvathā**
I. 1
IV. 79

सर्वधर्मन् : **sarvadharman**
II. 62

सर्वबुद्ध : **sarvabuddha**
VII. 34

सर्वभू : **sarvabhū**
(f)
VII. 39

सर्वभूमि : **sarvabhūmi**
VII. 30
VII. 41

सर्वरागिन् : **sarvarāgin**
VI. 9

सर्वविषय : **sarvaviṣaya**
VII. 3

सर्वशिक्षाव्यतिक्रम : **sarvaśikṣāvyati-krama**
IV. 34

सर्वसंग्रह : **sarvasaṃgraha**
I. 18

सर्वसत्व : **sarvasattva**
IV. 36

सर्वा
सर्व (स्त्री) : **sarvā**
(f)
I. 33
V. 66
V. 67
VII. 14

सर्वाङ्ग : **sarvāṅga**
IV. 36

सर्वापैर्निःशुभोऽष्टाभिर्विन्मनःकायजीवित : **sarvāpairnihśub-hoaṣtābhirvinm-anaḥkāyajīvita**
II. 20

सर्वालम्ब : **sarvālamba**
VII. 37

सर्वाविरोधित्व : **sarvāvirodhitva**
II. 30

सर्वास्तिवाद : **sarvāstivāda**
V. 25

सर्वास्रव : **sarvāstrava**
V. 65

सर्वे
सर्व (पुं) : **sarve**
III. 58
IV. 85
IV. 90
V. 19
V. 31
V. 56
VI. 19
VI. 69

सर्वै : **sarvaihi**
V. 24
V. 55

सर्वोभय : **sarvobhaya**
IV. 35

-सवस्तु- : **–savastu–**
VIII. 36

सवस्तुक : **savastuka**
I. 7

सवस्त्र : **savastra**
III. 70

सविचार : **savicāra**
IV. 7

सविपाक : **savipāka**
II. 10

सवितर्क : **savitarka**
I. 32

सवितर्कविचारोऽघः-समाधिः : **savitarkavicaro-sdhaḥsamadhi**
VIII. 23

सवितर्कविचारत्व : **savitarkvicartva**
II. 28

सविशेष : **saviśeṣa**
VI. 62

सविसंयोग : **savisaṃyoga**
II. 55

स्कन्ध : **skandha**
I. 8
I. 15
I. 25
III. 21
VIII. 2

स्कन्धमात्र : **skandhamātra**
III. 18

स्कन्धविघातविचिकित्सन : **skandhavighāta -vicikitsana**
V. 59

-स्कन्धा : **–skandhā**
(f)
VI. 19
VIII. 1

स्कन्धादी : **skandhādī**
I. 26

स्तूपभेदन : **stūpabhedana**
IV. 107

-स्तोत्र : **–stotra**
IV. 112

स्त्यान : **styāna**
II. 26
V. 47
V. 48
V. 51

स्त्यानौद्धत्यमद : **styānaudhatya -mada**
V. 53

स्त्री : **strī**
II. 12
II. 18
IV. 80
VIII. 3

-स्त्री- : **–strī–**
IV. 70

-स्त्री- : **–strī–**
VII. 6

स्त्रीन्द्रिय : **stīndriya**
II. 18

स्त्रीत्व : **stritva**
II. 2

स्त्रीपुरुषइन्द्रिये : **stripurusaindri ye**
II. 2

स्थान : **sthāna**
I. 8

-स्थान : **–sthāna**
III. 2
III. 72^2

स्थानास्थान : **sthānasthāna**
VII. 28

-स्थानिक : **–sthānika**
II. 72

स्थाप्य : **sthāpya**
V. 22

स्नेह : **sneha**
I. 12

स्पर्श : **sparśa**
II. 24
III. 30
III. 31^2

-स्पर्श- : **–sparśa–**
IV. 116

स्पर्शचेतनाविज्ञ : **sparśachetanāvi jña**
III. 40

स्प्रष्टव्य : **sprastvya**
I. 35
VII. 31

स्पृश्य : **spṛśya**
I. 10

स्पृहा : **spṛhā**
(f)
VI. 6

-स्पृहा : **–spṛhā**
IV. 77

हत : **hata**
I. 1

हरन्ति : **haranti**
ह
V. 40

हस्त : **hasta**
III. 87^2

हस्तचतुष्टय : **hastacatuṣtaya**
III. 87

हस्त्यादिसप्तकबल : **hastyādisaptak-abala**
VII. 31

हानभागाद्यनन्तर : **hānabhāgādyan -āntara**
VIII. 18

हानभागीय : **hānabhāgiya**
VIII. 17

हानि : **hāni**
(f)
VI. 22
VI. 58
VIII. 14

-हानि- : **–hāni–**
III. 42

-हानि : **–hāni**
III. 51
IV. 40^2

-हारिका : **–harikā**
IV. 106

हि : **hi**
I. 11
I. 17
I. 32
I. 45
II. 30
II. 45